Helping Your Depressed Teenager

Helping Your Depressed Teenager

A Guide for Parents
and Caregivers

Gerald D. Oster, Ph.D.
Sarah S. Montgomery, M.S.W.

JOHN WILEY & SONS, INC.

New York · Chichester · Brisbane · Toronto · Singapore

Copyright © 1995 by John Wiley & Sons, Inc.

Library of Congress Cataloging-in-Publication Data:

Oster, Gerald D.
 Helping your depressed teenager : a guide for parents and
caregivers / Gerald D. Oster, Sarah S. Montgomery.
  p. cm.
 Includes bibliographical references and index.
 ISBN 0-471-62184-6 (paper)
 1. Depression in adolescence. I. Montgomery, Sarah. II. Title.
RJ506.D40859 1995
 616.85'270083 dc
94-16197

Printed in the United States of America

10 9 8 7 6 5 4 3 2 1

Foreword

Only recently has it been widely accepted that children and adolescents can suffer from clinical depression. I clearly recall how, even during my medical internship in pediatrics in 1982, my suggestion that a young teenager seemed depressed generated criticism from the more experienced housestaff (as well as my receipt of a flurry of scientific reprints that explained why this could not be so). Wounded, but not discouraged, I continued to note the many children and teens who exhibited depression coincident with their medical problems, trying to find ways of helping them and of finding colleagues with an open mind on the subject. A residency opened in the psychiatry department, and my career in pediatrics gave way to the less scientifically precise but more personally suitable discipline of mental health.

So why is it that medical and mental health professionals, as well as the lay public, have taken so long to recognize and come to some consensus on a clinical problem that is right before their eyes? Perhaps it is because it has traditionally been so hard for adults to accept children and teenagers as individuals with real internal and adaptational conflicts that can lead to crisis and impaired development. Possibly, the recognition of emotional illness in children threatens to reflect on our deficiencies or uncertainties that parents deeply wish to hide. Indeed, it is sadly true that we find what we seek and we fail to notice that which is thought not to exist. In this regard, the frequently voiced adolescent sentiment, "Adults just don't have a clue about us," is conceivably accurate.

As a society, we prefer to think of our youth as happy, satisfied, supported, and having promising futures. It stands to reason that we would not wish to link our opinions of childhood and of mental illness in any way. It has been more comfortable and less incriminating of our culture's attitudes toward teenagers to view peculiar behaviors of adolescents as "passing life phases," "acting out," "boys being boys," or "teenage angst." Thus, we as adults might be exonerated of any wrongdoing—"It's them, not us."

v

Helping Your Depressed Teenager is a book well-suited for parents, families, and other concerned caretakers of preteens, teenagers, and even young adults. As a child and adolescent psychiatrist in active clinical practice, as well as a parent and concerned community member, I was pleased to be asked to write a foreword for this volume. In my close reading of this book, I was pleased at what its contents offer parents in terms of practical understanding of normal and abnormal adolescent development, of the psychopathology of depression and suicide, and of treatments and interventions.

The authors have covered a vast array of complex psychiatric literature and have presented it clearly, succinctly, and in plain language, with good case examples and sound suggestions for parents. I am hopeful that this publication will help those families struggling with teenage mood disorders by providing some support, clarification, and guidance. I further hope that it will lead to public awareness of the mental health needs of our youth, minimizing stigma and opening the door when needed to prompt evaluation and treatment by well-trained child psychiatrists, psychologists, and allied mental health clinicians.

BRIAN SIEGEL, M.D.
Private Practice and
University of Maryland School of Medicine
Baltimore, Maryland

Preface

Mary seems so tired and lethargic all the time; nothing excites her anymore.

Tyrone's become so withdrawn; he shuts himself in his room and refuses to talk with even his best friends.

We've found some poems in Michael's school notebook—all about darkness and death—that really scares us; my wife and I don't know what to think.

I can't tell if something is terribly wrong with Kim; she's acting so impossible. Or is she just being a teen?

These are the voices of actual parents, parents like you, who may be experiencing and wondering about changes in their teenagers. Many parents are aware of the pressures on their teens—from homes where financial strains create undue stress; from grades and career uncertainties, from the escalation of school violence; from the influence of peers, when fitting in may mean growing up too fast; and of course, from just being a teen.

Even the most well-intentioned parents can become anxious, weary, and sometimes even resentful of their teen when trying desperately to understand their teen's experience. These feelings can create multitudes of questions from parents and caregivers, about ways to seek help and whether effective treatments are available.

As a psychologist and a social worker, we, the authors, hear the stories, the confusion, and the pain. We strongly believe, however, that it is invaluable for you to be as educated and "in the know" as possible. With this book, we attempt to make a painful and confusing journey into a clearer and more hopeful one.

This book is about teenagers—your teen or the teen next door—who are showing depressed or angry feeling or who are perhaps contemplating suicide. We wrote this book as an educational guide for you, parents and caregivers, to understand the difference between the "normal" ups and downs of adolescence and the signs and symptoms of clinical depression. We also wrote it to help you gain awareness of the possible life-threatening signs of suicidal thoughts and feelings in teens and to provide assistance in navigating an often complex system of mental health treatment.

The teenage years are an invaluable time for physical and emotional growth, solidifying a sense of self and self-esteem, trying out rules, and realizing strengths and weaknesses. Most parents have the opportunity to watch their teens successfully move through the adolescent years without extended emotional upheaval. They watch their teenager develop a positive self-image and maintain close relationships with friends and peers. However, some parents may notice disturbing changes in their teen, such as being preoccupied with negative views and feelings, or voicing expressions of hopelessness, like "Life will never get better."

A distinct subgroup of teens do suffer from clinical depression, characterized by sad mood, low energy, loss of interests, and an uncaring facade. Often, these difficulties encountered in adolescence do not go away and may become serious disturbances in adulthood. More likely, these problems inhibit the development of personality, causing poor self-esteem, many self-doubts, and a propensity to give up easily when confronted with disappointment. And they also create an underachieving teen.

Being confronted by a teenager's sadness or anger can be puzzling, distressing, and certainly draining for all parents. In fact, one of the major problems in dealing with a teen's depressed feelings is the emotional upset it stirs up in parents. It is often said that we (parents, educators, and counselors) need to remind ourselves that we were probably not taught to deal with our own intense feelings during childhood. We were led to believe that to express such strong feelings was to be bad, and we were often made to feel guilty if we crossed the line of emotional acting out.

To respond effectively to a teenager who is moody and irritable, we need to have some clues about what may have caused the outbursts. Anger, for instance, may be a protection against painful feelings. It may also be a result of the frustration and failures of suffering from low self-esteem or loneliness. Feelings of depression and suicide may be expressed by teenagers who believe they have no control over their lives.

This is why this book was written—to bring you the knowledge and to share the experiences of teenagers. The book is a journey, from looking at the developmental tasks of every adolescent to focusing on those "risky" barriers during the teenage years that make certain youngsters prone to depression. It also looks at suicide, one very real risk of depression, and the cost and tragedies behind self-destructive actions. It discusses the process of seeking professional help, explaining individual and family therapy, the use of medication, and the possible need for hospitalization. The Appendix provides resources for parents and families with depressed adolescents, as well as organizations that focus on suicide prevention.

The fact that you are reading this book suggests that you want to become more aware of teenage depression and its consequences. It may mean that you want to reach out to someone in trouble. We hope this book assists you in that direction.

GERALD D. OSTER
SARAH S. MONTGOMERY

Olney, Maryland
Baltimore, Maryland
September 1994

Acknowledgments

Books always seem to have stories within stories. Although there is still some mystery about how they come to be on the bookshelves, there is no mystery about the number of people behind the scenes that add to the end product. So it is with the completion of this book.

For the stories to come alive and for the material to be collected and synthesized, many minds and hands, and much personal time have come together. To all those who have lent their expertise, their critical eye, and their supportive comments, we are grateful. For without those colleagues, friends, and family, our book would not be completed—it would exist as only ideas, images, and isolated pages waiting in vain to be pulled together.

There are so many people to whom we want to extend special recognition; however, time and space limits us to but a few. Our deep appreciation goes to Janice Caro, Ph.D., coauthor of the parallel professional book, *Understanding and Treating Depressed Adolescents and Their Families* (Wiley, 1990), and to her husband Richard Silver, who encouraged the endeavor of this book for parents. Thanks also goes to Peter LaCount, M.Ed., whose wonderful editing and patient understanding were indispensable. We also want to acknowledge Brian Siegel, M.D., for his assistance in clarifying some of the technical information on medication and for other supportive contributions. And special thanks goes to Beverly Bing and to Corriane.

There are also other people to whom we are grateful. The staff at Wiley, including Mary Daniello and Mintrue Gonzalez, have been a great help; Senior Editor Herb Reich offered us invaluable suggestions, as well as an encouraging and cheerful voice to get us through the laborious task of writing and rewriting. We also want to acknowledge the talent, workmanship, and enthusiasm of Jamie Temple and Maggie Dana from Pageworks who handled the design and typesetting, and Judith Cardanha, who handled the editing.

We would also like to recognize a few of the institutions that have made our work possible: the Regional Institute for Children and Adolescents in Rockville, Maryland; the Walter P. Carter Center in Baltimore; and Montgomery General Hospital in Olney. We would especially like to thank the staff at the University of Maryland Carruthers Clinic in Baltimore for their nourishment, humor, and support.

We are in privileged positions. During every day of our professional lives, others take us into their confidence to share their inner pain, personal struggles, and family secrets. Each story, each family, and each person is unique. One day we might hear the longing of a teenager struggling to be heard over his large family, the next day the anger of another who is hiding his misery by fighting and drinking. On the following day, we may be sitting with an adolescent who has been preoccupied with thoughts of hurting herself and has finally had the opportunity to share these thoughts. To these youngsters and their concerned families, we are truly indebted.

G.D.O.
S.S.M.

Contents

Helping Your Depressed Teenager

PART ONE

The Teenage Years

CHAPTER 1

On Becoming
a Teenager

Susan

Everyone liked Susan. At 16, she was active in the drama club, played field hockey, earned good grades, and had many friends. One morning, however, she came down for breakfast appearing tense and tearful. When her mother asked what was wrong, Susan would not even look at her. She just sat there, stared at her food, and did not pay attention to anything being said. She simply stated that she was not sick and just wanted to be left alone. Her mother was alarmed and confused. She had seen Susan like this before. Was this just another of Susan's mood swings that came on quickly and would be over just as suddenly? Or was this more serious? She was not so sure. Had anything happened? She took another look at her daughter hunched over her cereal and made a decision. She told Susan that it was okay for her to be alone for now, but that she was going to make a doctor's appointment. Susan just shrugged and went back upstairs to her room.

Harold

Harold, age 15, was even-tempered and well-mannered, but exceedingly shy. He had no close friends. After school, he always came home immediately. He never went to parties. He attempted to date but felt miserable and embarrassed by his inability to carry on a conversation. He quit trying.

One fall, he got up the courage to try out for basketball but did not make the team. After that, he did not try other sports, even though he was a pretty good athlete. He never said much about it, but quietly he was hurting. He secretly wished he was more outgoing, but he feared possible rejection. He was afraid and frustrated over his inability to overcome his shyness.

Harold kept his feelings to himself, especially his anger, and was rarely moody. No one ever complained about him or even thought much about him. No one ever reached out to him to discover what was behind his blank facade. While his peers were hanging out with each other, going to parties, talking on the telephone, and beginning to date, he stayed at home and read. As such, he never practiced the social skills that they were learning. He seemed to merely exist. Yet behind his expressionless mask, he was crying, tormented, and very much alone. Finally, a caring and sensitive uncle directed Harold to a counselor who helped him out of his emotional shell. As a result, Harold felt like he was coming out of exile and began to enjoy life.

Joe

Joe, age 17, was a highly creative and intelligent young man who was outgoing but incessantly moody. Sometimes he was sad and sullen, sometimes full of life and energy, and sometimes intensely angry. These extreme mood changes made him feel out of control, and sometimes he would think about hurting himself or someone else. These thoughts frightened him and made him feel extremely anxious. He began drinking to dampen the pain—first a little, then to excess. He also used drugs when they were available, usually at the parties he so often attended. Alarmed by his mood swings and failing grades in school and afraid of drug use, his parents brought Joe to the adolescent evaluation unit of a psychiatric hospital. Joe was diagnosed as having a bipolar mood disorder and treated accordingly. He was then able to return to his home and school. With outpatient therapy and prescribed medication, he was finally able to use the many abilities he possessed.

THE TEENAGE YEARS

The teenage (or adolescent) years can be exciting and adventuresome, yet they can also be confusing and full of conflict. Although many adults remember these years as carefree and fun, just as many are relieved to have put this period of their life behind them. With the onset of puberty, teenagers must cope with considerable emotional, mental, and physical changes. They must learn to (a) adapt to a changing body, (b) handle intensified feelings, (c) deal with sexual relations, and (d) forge an identity that is separate from their parents and approved by their peers. Those are just several of the normal developmental tasks that teenagers must handle.

Because teenagers are changing rapidly, they are constantly reexamining themselves, renegotiating their friendships, and questioning their values. They are frequently comparing themselves to their peers and to the "ideal" teen presented by television programs, movies, and commercials. This frequently leaves them vulnerable, self-conscious, and full of self-doubt. Although most teenagers can navigate through these pushes and pulls without too much wavering, many find them overwhelming and act out their distress. This *acting out* can take the form of (a) constantly testing the limits and standards established by their parents, (b) arguing over nothing, (c) losing interest in their prior activities (as distractions increase and peers become increasingly important), and (d) using drugs or alcohol to subdue the intensity of their feelings.

A TIME OF RAPID CHANGE

Each change must be examined and accepted if a teenager is to progress into a satisfactory and productive adulthood.

Bodily Changes

With the onset of puberty, teenagers must confront dramatic physical and hormonal changes. Growth spurts in height and weight are common. This rapid growth often causes clumsiness that leads to embarrassment and self-consciousness. Today, teenagers are also reaching puberty at an earlier age (often as early as 11 years old). This early onset of puberty increases the gap between physical and emotional maturity, leaving younger adolescents even more at risk for confusion and low self-esteem.

Emerging Sexuality

In addition to growth spurts, teenagers must deal with the maturation of their sexual and reproductive organs. Because of the different rates of maturation, comparisons are inevitable. Teenagers who develop unusually early or late are likely to receive negative feedback about their physical attractiveness and abilities. Additionally, research suggests that about half of all teenagers have sexual intercourse before graduating from high school. Sex and its possible consequences (i.e., pregnancy, threat of sexually transmitted diseases, etc.) can create many additional pressures that can cause heightened anxiety and self-doubt and interfere with growth towards a healthy adulthood.

Teenagers also may have concerns about their sexual fantasies and sexual orientation. Though most of the media images and environmental cues presume heterosexuality, some adolescents have attractions and feelings towards same-sex partners. The pressure to conform and behave like the heterosexual majority can cause a great deal of stress and anxiety in some teenagers.

Identity Formation

Identity is the sense of one's special place (or niche) in the world. Teenagers are constantly trying to discover who they are, who they will become, and where they belong. To find out, they experiment with various social roles, and with different behaviors, clothes, and even ways of speaking. During this time, teenagers are very sensitive to criticism and rejection. They especially need acceptance and understanding from their parents and other important adults. These same adults might have only recently solidified their own identity and might have difficulty understanding and accepting the constant change and instability that this experimentation brings. Thus, a generation gap begins.

Everyday Stress

Teenagers are rarely taught ways to deal with the daily pressures they experience. Although many adults are coming to realize that stressors of daily activity do take tolls on health, they often fail to acknowledge that their children are also affected. It is sometimes difficult to realize after a frustrating day of work that your child may also be feeling vulnerable and frazzled!

Increases in physical complaints, unpleasant feelings, and behavior change are often observed in teenagers when stressed. In extreme cases, teenagers can develop emotional illnesses as eating disorders (such as anorexia nervosa or bulimia) when their internal pressures are heightened without available or appropriate releases. Too much stress can also cause serious damage to a teenager's self-esteem, which can lead to depression and, if left unchecked, to the possibility of suicide.

Family Values

The teenage years usually come at a time when parents have become firm in their own identities. Values ultimately begin to clash and communication problems between parents and their teenage children begin to arise. Few parents have either the time or energy to be patient and listen to the feelings being expressed by their children, especially when the teen is angry or upset.

The absence of parental involvement and attention only increases the risk for emotional upheaval. It is no wonder that in today's fast-paced world, increases in physical, sexual, and emotional abuse have been reported. There also have been dramatic increases in divorce rates and in the number of single-parent households. The "blended" family is becoming the norm. Combined, these changes and conflicts add to the feelings of insecurity and internal confusion already being experienced by the teenagers.

Separation from Family

During adolescence, young men and women often struggle between needing their families and wanting to be independent. They vacillate between listening to their parents and listening to their peers. This wavering creates confusion and inconsistency in their reasoning and behavior. It is no wonder that most teenagers are viewed just as "mixed-up kids"—they are! Even those teenagers who leave home for college often experience mixed feelings and seem to behave erratically.

Many graduating high school seniors and incoming college freshman experience brief periods of sadness and depression and may need additional emotional support during this transition. It is important that they be made aware that their reactions to new environments and their feelings are normal. Parents need to give their departing young adults approval to seek help from their college counseling center or other campus support networks.

MAJOR TASKS TO ACCOMPLISH

To become a functional adult, one must let go of childhood dependencies and become independent and responsible for oneself and others. This is not an easy process. The transitional period of adolescence allows teenagers the necessary time to: (a) learn to provide for themselves, (b) decide on appropriate work and to begin developing the skills required for that work, (c) clarify their own values and beliefs, (d) learn to relate intimately (not necessarily sexually) with other people, (e) discover their own strengths and weaknesses, and (f) learn to accept themselves for what they are and are not.

These tasks of development are not accomplished all at once or by a certain age. Yet for parents and other concerned adults, these tasks can be utilized as a "road map" to better understand teenagers and their actions.

Each milestone must be successfully negotiated to make a successful transition into adulthood. If teens experience too many failures, doubts, and uncertainties in their tasks, they are blocked from developing normally. Ultimately, this can lead to extreme moodiness, inconsistency in relationships, and reactions against rules and regulations, all of which may undermine a teenager's self-esteem and contribute to periods of depression and despair.

THE INFLUENCE OF PEERS

To make the transition from childhood to adulthood successfully, teenagers must continually question many of their earlier ideas and assumptions. They must practice new ways of thinking, feeling, and appearing. Because their old ways of dealing with the world were largely acquired from parents and other significant adults, teenagers must now direct much of their resistance and questioning toward these very same figures. Teenagers still need approval and confirmation, however, so they must look to peers for support of these new experimental ways of thinking, feeling, and behaving.

The peer group serves the important function of being the arena for trying on new masks and disguises, and it lessens the reliance on significant adults for feedback. Within a teenager's peer group, (a) new norms are discovered, (b) emotional support is sought and given in the striving for independence, (c) companionship is provided, and (d) modeling is displayed for age-appropriate behaviors.

The need to be with friends, as opposed to parents, is most powerful in younger and middle adolescents (the 12- to 15-year olds). These younger adolescents attempt, by whatever means necessary, to remain in close contact with their friends in order to discover how and where they fit into this new extended family and support system. Children this age feel a paramount need to know what is going on and to see how everyone feels about an issue. Group conformity and loyalty play a formidable role.

Teenagers base much of their self-concept and self-confidence on where they find themselves in their peer group. Although teenagers strive to find their own identities outside their family, the thought of being different is generally *not* valued by teenagers. It becomes essential for them to do what others in their age bracket are doing, whether it is wearing similar clothing, talking the same language, or hanging out in a popular setting.

As a matter of fact, doing the same thing as everyone else is more highly regarded by adolescents than adults. Doing "one's own thing" is actually doing what a particular peer group currently values. While this behavior may be seen as immature by adults, it is perceived as very mature by teenagers, especially younger adolescents. Fortunately, as these same teens become older and more self-reliant, their need to gain acceptance and validation from peers lessens.

PARENTAL VIEWS OF PEER ACCEPTANCE

As a parent, you are certain to have many mixed feelings when observing your youngster turning increasingly toward peers for support and advice. The process of adolescence is not a steady course away from parents. Teens alternate between periods of wanting to lean on their parents and periods of wanting to pull away from them. It becomes essential during this time to let your teens know that you are available to listen whenever they are ready to talk. This message must be given with the idea that you will not criticize but will attempt to understand and support them.

Teenagers must have some way to test the accuracy of their own perceptions and reflections—an important role for an encouraging but not overly involved parent. Because teens naturally resist parental authority and advice, it is best to reserve advice for those times when they ask for it directly.

The more you are able to listen to teenagers without preaching, lecturing, or telling them what they should do, the more likely it is that they will recognize that you are not trying to undermine their move toward independence. With this trust, they will be freer to initiate communication and interaction.

Letting teenagers keep their silence is okay, too. They may need some time to do their own thinking without your input for awhile. Sometimes, try being a sounding board instead of an advice giver.

THINGS TO REMEMBER

- Adolescence is a time of rapid change—bodies are changing, emotions are intensifying, and peers are becoming increasingly important.
- There are many hurdles for teens to overcome before they take on the responsibilities of the adult world. Try to remember what it was like for you to navigate through your teen years.
- Try to listen to your teenager supportively rather than to give a liberal amount of advice. Save advice for times when your teen asks for your input.
- It is a natural part of adolescence for teens to show they are separate from their parents—often they choose clothes, language, and interests that say "I am different" from my parents. In some ways, they are going through another "terrible twos" stage; but, instead of relying on a monosyllabic "no," they are differentiating themselves in other ways.
- A teen's looking toward peers for support should not be a threat to your authority. Adolescents need this time to discover who they are and how they fit into the larger picture.

CHAPTER 2

Today's Teenagers: Is There Something Wrong?

Tanika

Tanika was an almost 17-year-old young woman admitted to the psychiatric unit of a community hospital. Although she had been in outpatient therapy for two years, her symptoms of depression had increased. Recently, she had expressed thoughts of suicide. Over the several months preceding hospitalization, she had experienced eating and sleeping problems, and declining grades; she continuously argued with her family; and, on occasion, she had run away. Previously, she had been an honors student and quite active in her church.

Sean

For many years, Sean had been treated for hyperactivity and learning problems. His self-esteem had suffered tremendously. Now a teenager, Sean still had problems in controlling his behaviors and emotions. He was more sensitive than ever. More arguments and fights ensued. Only after a school counselor asked him what he was really feeling did Sean allow anyone to look behind his mask of rage and see his tears.

Maria

Maria had had a volatile year requiring three separate psychiatric hospitalizations. On two occasions, she threatened her parents—once with a butcher knife. Another time, after an argument, she consumed nearly an entire bottle of aspirin. Although enrolled in the 11th grade, she rarely attended school, stating "I just want to stay in my room . . . I don't like school." According to her parents, she had recently been involved with a slightly older crowd who had already dropped out of school and were using drugs.

ADDED RISK FACTORS

Since the late 1960s, a number of factors—including geographic, economic, and familial changes—have made the period of adolescence (from approximately the age of 12 years to 18 years) especially risky for teenagers and their families. Teenagers are frequently confronted with fears about the possibility of divorce within their own or a friend's family. Overcrowded schools have led to impersonal atmospheres that create feelings of estrangement from peers and adults. Feelings of alienation and aloneness create within teenagers an air of mistrust that often makes them more susceptible to feelings of rejection, which can seriously impair their self-concept and undermine their confidence.

These lost avenues of communication may inhibit the possibility of forming close, meaningful relationships. These relationships provide the necessary feedback from peers and significant adults that help teenagers adjust to their eventual separation from parents and their impending independence. This breakdown in feedback has been implicated by some researchers as an important missing link that may lead to teenage depression and suicide attempts.

Signs of significant depression have characterized teenage populations in increasing numbers during the past 25 years. These symptoms have included sudden changes in everyday functioning, as reflected by decreased peer activity and declining grades. Additionally, those teenagers who seem easily overwhelmed or rageful have been noted as experiencing bouts of underlying depression.

The use of alcohol and other drugs has increased so dramatically during this period that it has now become a major public health problem in this country and around the world. Although teenagers may be using alcohol and drugs to defend themselves against the unpleasant feelings accompanying anxiety and depression, it is these very same substances that may disinhibit the urge to attempt suicide.

PRESSURES TO ACHIEVE

Today's world places a premium on achievement and competition. Academic success may pave the road to the good and luxurious life. Good grades and high test scores can mean going to the "right" college. Parents may have unrealistic expectations for success at a time when some teenagers may not be ready for the pressures placed on them by those expectations. This can cause damage to a teenager's sense of selfworth and ultimately damage his or her self-esteem.

Overachieving teenagers, on the other hand, seem driven to excel. They are characteristically seen as always being on the go, trying to be the best, and taking on too many responsibilities. These teenagers pride themselves on their intellect and on their logical reasoning. They are driven to succeed and try fiercely to be independent.

However, overachievers are actually very dependent on outside accomplishments to justify their existence. The more academic and social successes they achieve, the better others will view them; the greater the successes, the better teens feel toward themselves. These achievements validate them as superior.

Because of their intellect and energy, overachieving teenagers find success for a time and feel "on top of the world." But, when they realize that perfection is impossible, they feel let down and frustrated.

SUPPORTING YOUR OVERACHIEVER

Unfortunately, many parents do not realize that these superteens feel as dependent as other teens—they, too, need support, but they usually do not get it because they appear successful on the outside and refuse to ask for assistance. They possess superior ability to reason and to make excuses, and they tend to rationalize any weakness that is pointed out to them.

Overachieving teens rarely express their genuine feelings, especially anger. Negative feelings may seem so unacceptable that they bottle them up, not usually expressing them in everyday conversation or activity.

When such feelings do occasionally surface, the teens believe they are guilty of some impropriety for having these thoughts or feelings. When intense feelings cannot be outwardly expressed, they are sometimes directed inward, causing other feelings of alienation and of being unloved.

When unfortunate circumstances occur, such as failure or rejection, overachieving teenagers often react in a manner completely opposite to what would be expected of them. For examples, on the night of high school graduation, the class valedictorian commits suicide or, faced with the ensuing stressors of college, a bright youngster drops out from academic pursuits entirely.

Parents must be aware of what is considered a well-balanced life for a teenager and intervene on their teenager's behalf when they see an imbalance. Overachieving teens go to great lengths to avoid embarrassing situations; they do not want to see their weaknesses exposed. When parents confront them, they may become irritable and disagree with their parents' arguments even more. However, conviction and sincerity on a parent's part will be heard and appreciated by the teen.

If a parent is supportive of a teenager on an emotional level, he or she sends a message of understanding and of being available to the teen on his or her terms. Most of all, the parent has told the son or daughter "I know you are human and are struggling just like everyone." Teenagers are secretly delighted to have their parents on their side.

ARE TODAY'S TEENS LESS HEALTHY THAN THEIR PARENTS?

Recently, a national commission of educators and doctors was formed to make recommendations on the role of the school and the community in improving adolescent health. The panel consensus suggested that teenagers of today are less healthy than their parents. It pointed to the alarming increases in unwanted pregnancies, illegal drug use, suicide, and violence as justifications for their concerns. The statistics showed the following:

- One million teenage girls—nearly 1 in 10—get pregnant each year.
- Thirty-nine percent of high school seniors reported that they had gotten drunk within the two previous weeks.

• Alcohol-related accidents are the leading cause of death among teen-agers.

• The suicide rate for teens has doubled since 1968, making it one of the leading causes of death among adolescents. Ten percent of teenage boys and 18 percent of girls have attempted suicide.

• The number of arrests of adolescents is 30 times greater than in 1950.

• Homicide is the leading cause of death among minority youths ages 15 to 19.

The commission concluded that the lack of attention paid to these problems has left thousands of young people doomed to failure, "which for many will be a precursor to an adult life of crime, unemployment or welfare dependency." The cochairperson of the panel, which was formed by the National Association of State Boards of Education and the American Medical Association, stated that unless action was taken immediately the country would be faced with a "failing economy and social unrest." Suggestions were presented to establish adolescent health centers in schools or other locations frequented by teenagers to be financed by both public and private funds. The commission also proposed a multifaceted health education program that should be implemented in all schools.

AN EVOLVING WORLD?

To give some idea of the changed world teenagers face today, a listing was compiled by the Fullerton, California, Police Department and the California Department of Education that contrasted the top nonscholastic concerns in public schools during 1940 and again in 1982. During the 1940s, students' problems focused on running in the halls, chewing gum, talking out of turn, wearing inappropriate clothes, and not staying in line. The identical survey administered in the 1980s found such problems as alcohol and drug abuse, pregnancy, suicide, assault, and gang warfare as the most salient issues impeding educational progress! The 1990s have found these problems even more intensified. Certainly the world is evolving (whether positively or negatively is left to discussion), but with the evolution comes the pressures to reconcile the tension caused by the changes.

Are teenagers truly capable of coping with today's stresses? It seems that the teenage years have always been an accurate reflection of society's changing morals and values, and teenagers themselves react to these challenges and pressures in ways that range from the creative to the destructive. In fact, recent research by developmental psychologists has shown that for most teenagers (about 80 present), these years are fulfilling and enjoyable. This still leaves 20 present (or 3.4 million teenagers) who view life as problematic and who struggle to find satisfying ways of handling their stress.

WHAT PARENTS MUST DO

Listen to Your Teenagers

Listen to your teenagers when they talk to you and when their friends talk to you. You do not have to be a spy—just stay alert. If after every weekend you hear jokes about who was "smashed," you know there is a lot of drinking going on. One young boy just happened to pick up the extension when his 15-year-old brother was on the phone planning an afternoon at a friend's house. "Bring some booze; we are all out," he heard the friend say. The older brother said he could not get anything from the liquor cabinet because too many people were around. The younger boy told his mother. (Whether he should have or not is a decision each family has to make.) She picked up her older son earlier than planned and talked with him calmly about what his friends were doing. She had no idea before this that they spent Saturday afternoons drinking.

Do Not Deny the Obvious

It is unrealistic to think that your child can slide through adolescence without being exposed to alcohol and drugs, no matter where you live. Drugs seem available everywhere, with the average age of first use now hovering around 12 years of age and dropping. More than 3 million problem drinkers in this country are under the legal drinking age. Problem drinking is often associated with drug use, school problems, and teenage pregnancy, forming a devastating combination.

The world is everchanging. In 1962, fewer than 4 percent of the population had tried an illicit drug; now, 57 percent have tried at least one drug before they graduate from high school. These are not necessarily the kids who "look funny," easily identified by their schoolmates as "the druggies" or "the boozers." They are also the athletes, the successful students, and the class presidents, the good kids who just a few years ago were assumed to be immune from drugs. A New York State study of students in grades 7 to 12 in 1983 showed that, contrary to public opinion, the affluent Hudson River suburbs, not New York City, had the highest percentage of youngsters using drugs.

A CONCLUDING QUESTION AND ANSWER

"Everytime I hear my daughter scream, 'You don't understand me,' I get angry, but I also feel helpless in getting through to her," a parent says. "How can I make her understand me?"

How very often parents hear "You don't understand me," and how very hard it is not to get upset and become embroiled in a no-win battle. When teenagers make this or similar statements, you must consider that they are frightened and are feeling so confused that they do not believe anyone can understand them, even their own parent(s). Parents often become defensive, feeling they are being personally attacked for not doing something to relieve their youngster's pain and distress.

The next time your teenager directs his or her anger at you, stop and ask in a calm manner, "Why are you feeling this way?" or "What is going on with you at this moment that is causing you so much frustration?" This approach usually works better than trying to counter with a statement like "Of course I understand you; I am your parent," or some other comeback in a similar argumentative tone.

The answer may be forthcoming and hold surprises. Do not ever assume you know all the factors surrounding your teenager's dilemma. Directing their exclamation back onto them in a calm manner will produce the groundwork for reassurance from you (something all teenagers need and want) and a more meaningful dialogue for the future.

All too often teenagers express their internal pressure in ways that parents find difficult to tolerate—angry outbursts and withdrawal from the family, for example. Parents who learn to read these kinds of behaviors as expressions of frustration and inner turmoil can be more available to help their teenagers develop healthy and creative coping strategies.

There also may be times when your teenager does not have much to say or cannot say it in an appropriate manner. What parents need to do is to listen and acknowledge their teenager's opinions and feelings. Comforting comments that show understanding are usually all that they are looking for—not for you to tell them how to make things "right." It becomes important to let your children know that you are available to listen with understanding and support whenever they are ready to talk.

Because teenagers naturally resist parental authority and advice, it is best to reserve advice for those times when they ask for it directly. The more you are able to listen to teenagers without preaching or "lecturing," the more they will recognize that you are helping them move toward independence. Only then will your teenager feel better about talking to you.

THINGS TO REMEMBER

- Growing up in today's world does present new challenges for both teenagers and their parents, but it also presents opportunities for creative responses.
- Even kids who seem on top of the world need guidance and support. Their emotional needs should not be neglected.
- Even during these troublesome times, most youths do enjoy their teenage years and are able to successfully navigate through these years.
- Parents need to be aware of and to empathize with their teenagers' problems.
- Try to understand what your teenagers are really trying to say. Get them to help you understand. The burden is on them to communicate, not for you to read their minds.

CHAPTER 3

The Early Teen Years: Are They Truly a Wonder?

NEW AWAKENINGS

With the onset of puberty, children's worlds are no longer predictable and structured. Almost overnight, bodily changes cast them into adult-like statuses. Societies place increasingly greater demands on them and expect obedience to general rules and regulations. Growth spurts occur, and interests and friendships are pursued based on new physical characteristics.

Outward behavior may reflect these dramatic and uneven changes. Wide mood swings may become the norm. Younger teenagers may be energized one minute, and lethargic the next. They may engage in prolonged day-dreaming. Previously agreeable children may become argumentative. Many times, parents are caught off guard and are not prepared for this onslaught by their once even-tempered, good-natured child. For many families, conflict becomes an everyday occurrence.

EARLY ADOLESCENCE

For 12-years-olds, activities are primarily shared with same-sex peers. Special friendships are often made that are paramount to them until something goes wrong in the relationship. Although many 12-year-olds keep their moods and feelings to themselves, they do tend to be especially sensi-

19

tive to interpersonal slights. This may cause verbal and even physical attacks on others when feelings are hurt.

As can be expected, parents must anticipate managing hurt feelings and helping their youngsters make up after a fight. This is especially important because this is a time for the likely transition from elementary to middle school. Moving into a larger secondary school usually changes the structure of peer groups and friendships. These changes can add to the stresses of early teens and create much inner conflict and confusion for them. As they begin establishing new contacts, they are susceptible to many criticisms from peers and may need extra support from adults.

In contrast, at age 13, most young teenagers start becoming introspective. When feelings are hurt, they usually withdraw. Many begin to worry about school performance; some may try to study harder while others may not complete assignments for fear of failing to meet their teachers' expectations. During this period, gender stereotypical play and interests seem to be common—boys may reject certain activities or school subjects as feminine; girls may avoid those subjects, such as math, that they view as unfeminine.

SEXUAL MATURATION AND DATING

By the time adolescents reach 14 or 15, many more of their activities involve the opposite sex. Dating becomes a time for high anxiety for both teenagers and their parents. Boys become worried about asking girls out and become nervous about possible rejection. "Does she like me? What if she laughs out loud and hangs up the phone?" Girls become preoccupied about being asked out and what to expect on a date. They may feel confusion over whether it is acceptable for girls to initiate a relationship.

Although these problems tend to smooth themselves out over time and with practice, the extent of sexual activity during this early dating period is often of great concern to both boys and girls. The degree of sexual involvement also is related to the partner's age and experience, though much depends on cultural, familial, and personal values. Thus, if the partner is older or more experienced, there is a greater likelihood of sexual intimacy.

Sexual maturation also produces much worry during early adolescence and heightens anxiety and self-consciousness. For both boys and girls, there are vast concerns that rapid bodily changes will produce less than desirable results. Besides a preoccupation that they will be too large or too short, attractive or not, there is much anxiety directed towards their sexuality.

For girls, there is much fear that something may be wrong if their periods are irregular. They may fear pregnancy regardless of sexual activity. Misinformation about sex can cause countless unfounded worries. Sexual fantasies can cause reactions of panic and guilt. This creates much embarrassment and uneasiness for younger adolescent girls and can result in inner turmoil and distractions that can hinder their effective growth and development.

For boys, erections at inopportune moments become a major source of embarrassment and worry. Keeping other people from noticing can be a major concern, as well as keeping their mothers from noticing that they have emissions while sleeping. Also, most boys masturbate, and their experiences may produce feelings of guilt or confusion about the consequences. Even information about masturbation may become misleading if it is vague. How is a young man supposed to make sense of statements such as, "Masturbation is normal unless carried to excess?"

ACCURATE SEXUAL INFORMATION

These years can be particularly troubling for adolescent boys and girls who find themselves predominantly attracted to their same sex. Some predominantly heterosexual youth may have fantasies or crushes on members of the same sex, which can lead to feelings of confusion and guilt.

A significant percentage of youth (possibly 10%) are predominantly attracted to members of the same sex. These sexual-minority youths may feel extreme anxiety or concern about being "different" and may worry about being ostracized from their families and communities. Often, these teens wear a mask of heterosexuality, dating members of the opposite sex and sharing stories of sexual interludes to conform to outward expectations, while feeling intensely alone and vulnerable inside.

All adolescents are highly interested in sex and accurate sexual information. Boys are exposed to scrutiny about the size of their penises and may be quite concerned about performing sexually. Girls may worry about the size and shape of their growing breasts and may feel self-conscious about needing to wear a bra. Jokes about bodily parts and functions become common and may leave both boys and girls feeling very vulnerable during this time.

Also of concern for younger adolescents is the impression they make on each other. As advertisers are broadcasting what look is desirable, parents and other important figures may be saying that appearances do not matter. Since mixed messages like this are common during this time period, it can lead to much confusion, doubt, and uncertainty.

THE MIDDLE TEEN YEARS

Maturity

The intense preoccupations of the early teenage years seem to diminish somewhat when teens grow older. This seems to occur as they gain some degree of experience and perspective in their interpersonal relationships. Although many teenagers still feel somewhat dissatisfied with the results of their physical growth or have been slow to develop and mature, most have attained satisfactory and acceptable results. Their countless questions about their height, weight, and sexual characteristics have now been somewhat resolved.

Height and weight increase more slowly during this time, and any physical clumsiness or disproportions in growth usually correct themselves during this period. Secondary sex characteristics have typically shown by the middle teen years, though the sex organs may not be fully mature until the end of this period. Skin problems like acne or excessively oily hair may become of increasing concern for middle adolescents.

If everything is going relatively well for the teenager, he or she is beginning to solidify an identity and beginning to practice adultlike roles and responsibilities. By this time, there is usually an improvement in family relations, as the teenager is beginning to express his or her wants and needs in a more appropriate manner. This reduction in familial stress can lead on to a more harmonious ending of these years as the teenager prepares to leave home.

Milestones Toward Independence

There are, however, certain pitfalls during this time. Driving a car can lead to exasperation for both adolescent and parent and create much anxiety and turmoil. Adolescents see driving as a symbol of their independence. Parents, however, have varied reactions. Some do view it as a major step towards their son or daughter entering adulthood. They certainly look forward to the day when they are no longer their son's or daughter's chauffeur!

Other parents, however, view it as a source of tension. Arguments ensue about sharing the family car or about being responsible enough to drive at this age. These conflicts are especially volatile if the teenager is no longer doing his or her share of the chores, doing poorly in school, or violating household rules.

Automobiles also symbolize what parents most fear giving their teenagers—freedom and privacy. Just when parents are beginning to worry the most about their teenagers' actions or friends, now their teenagers have a way of becoming very evasive. Of course, there is also the grave concern about accidents; and, in fact, car accidents are one of the leading causes of teenage deaths.

Jobs for teenagers also have become a matter of mixed blessings. On the one hand, they are valuable in regard to extra household income and trying out adult roles and responsibilities; on the other hand, the jobs may not leave enough time for school achievement or adequate rest. Tensions and frustrations may ensue.

Like all workers, teenagers may encounter disappointments about the feedback they receive or become disillusioned about the job itself. This may cloud their expectations for further work pursuits or undermine their confidence at a time when they need praise for their efforts. A moderate degree of job experience, however, can be extremely beneficial in beginning to understand the world of work. Teens gain skills in appreciating and managing money. It also becomes a time to test skills and to discover what is personally satisfying about a possible adult job.

Love and Sex

Love attachments during this time period can be precarious. Teenagers will experience many highs and lows as they "practice" various forms of sexual expression. Although many crushes may appear foolish to adults, these crushes do serve crucial functions for the developing teenager. They can help adolescents discover what characteristics they prefer in other people, and they can help adolescents learn appropriate interpersonal skills. This kind of relationship should not ordinarily cause a major problem unless the involvement becomes overly intense or explicit. For parents to reject these overtures to "falling in love" or to fail to recognize them as a natural stepping stone into adulthood can result in emotional turmoil by their teenage children.

Relationships within one's peer group moves along a line from (a) showing up at an "in spot" (b) to pairing off for social events (c) to group dating (d) to single-couple dating. During middle adolescence, teenagers often prefer the group dating over single dating. Group dating allows more teens to participate, including those teens without cars or those whose parents are concerned about them riding with a recently licensed driver.

Many teenagers want to date a single individual because this provides them with security and social approval. Of course, parents may associate this kind of dating with increased sexual activity, pregnancy, and sexually transmitted diseases. Teens' misinformation about practicing safe sexual methods is common. Also, each partner may expect the other to use contraceptives when neither of them are doing so. Many teens, like many adults, lack the communication skills and the social confidence to negotiate this issue with their partners.

Signs of Emotional Expression

On an emotional level, these middle teenagers are somewhat less likely to lose their tempers, although they may regress when exceptionally frustrated. These teenagers begin to interpret the world more maturely and to express their emotions more adeptly.

Anger, a common response to frustration at this age, may now begin to be expressed by temper outbursts such as yelling or extreme moodiness rather than by throwing things or fighting. By this time, expressions of anger may be delayed because the adolescent is learning better methods of impulse control. Sometimes, however, parents may experience the brunt of their teenager's pent-up anger and are left wondering what offense led to such an outburst.

Grief may be deeply experienced but tightly concealed by midteen adolescents. When loss is confronted, parents may puzzle at their teens' lack of recognizable signs of mourning; however, the teenagers' hurt and fear may produce opposite reactions, such as making light of their or other's feelings of loss. By attempting to emotionally remove themselves, these teenagers are merely trying to hide their deep hurt and lessen their own sense of inadequacy in responding to the loss.

Teenagers do experience many inadequacies, but try to hide them at all costs. They worry about everything but deny this "weakness" through statements like "I don't care, it doesn't faze me." Even though they are worried about many issues that can be discussed with many caring adults, they fail to take advantage of this and have difficulty in asking for assistance.

Sometimes they may approach adults through questions about a friend, and the adult needs to be sensitive for these signs of seeking aid and to respond in a subtle manner. Adults cued into this indirect way of asking for help can provide a strong platform and sounding board for many unanswered questions.

Hiding Behind Their Masks

When children find themselves becoming teenagers, they no longer want to see themselves as dependent on their parents. With their urgency to let go from their major source of self-esteem, that is, their families, they are likely to experience a bumpy ride. Trying to find ready replacements for their main source of love and attention, they tend to move in and out of relationships quickly. They may also expect more from themselves than their abilities will actually allow.

Teenagers battle their fears constantly, becoming elated when victorious and very down when defeated. These mood swings produce inconsistency in their subsequent actions. To overcome feelings of self-doubt or shame, teenagers attempt to show their parents that nothing is actually wrong. They often use disguises or masks to hide their underlying feelings.

Not Wanting Help

Teenagers will often do anything rather than say they need help from adults. They may go out of their way to hide their fears and doubts about themselves. This avoidance may make it hard for adults to reach out to them.

Feelings and Reactions

Teenagers do not always understand the reasons why they feel a certain way. They readily blame others or events for their moods. Comments such as "School is boring" or "That teacher is a drag" are commonplace. Teenagers are often not aware that their internal feelings are setting the tone for their reactions and preferences.

Seeking Distractions

Teenagers often actively attempt to avoid confronting their unpleasant feelings by looking for excitement and distractions. They try to stay one step ahead of their sadness or anxiety. This may lead to excessive behaviors like using drugs or running away that may end up causing even greater problems.

Working Too Hard

Some teenagers will try to cover sad feelings by trying to overachieve. They believe that if they work hard and achieve more, their bad feelings will magically vanish. However, even minor slips may make them feel as though their positions and beliefs are shaky, leaving them vulnerable to feelings of insecurity.

FOR PARENTS

Being alert to the signs and disguises of teenagers' actual feelings will go a long way in helping them adjust to these shaky years. If your teenager or any friends of your teenager ask for even a little bit of help, take the request seriously. Your intervention could mean a great deal in changing their lives. Teenagers are not always what they appear to be. Though they may hide behind a mask of an "I don't care" shrug, most teens do need a guiding and supportive hand.

THINGS TO REMEMBER

- At a time when parents expect their children to finally have control, teenagers' bodies are often out of control.
- Outward behavior is usually a reflection of inner changes and conflicts.
- Sexual maturation will be an anxious time both for your developing teen and for you.
- Teenagers need information on sex that is both relevant and accurate.
- Independence brings with it both freedoms and tensions.
- Teenagers wear many masks. It is often helpful to think about what are behind those disguises.

CHAPTER 4

Graduation and Beyond

LEAVING HOME

Bidding Farewell to the Teenage Years

Bidding adieu to parents and family, and packing bags and heading off to work or college can evoke as much sadness and uncertainty as excitement. The soon-to-be-adult child may experience a kaleidoscope of feelings, hopes, and expectations as well as fears, insecurities, and pains of separation. Parents, bragging to all who will listen about their teenager's accomplishments, may harbor fears and losses as well.

The family constellation is about to change and the remaining members are faced with the need to readjust their role expectations. Questions and doubts may arise—Who will now mow the lawn? Who will take care of the twins during bridge night? What will it be like to hear the empty space of a silent phone? On another level, sometimes the departing teenager has been a confidant for one of the parents, and the parent begins to wonder who will replace this loss.

In the past, much psychological theory and research on this transitional phase into adulthood has focused on the teenager's inner world. The young adult preparing to leave home is thrust into a position of self-discovery as he or she becomes concerned about such matters as (a) the need for dependence while wanting to be independent, (b) solidification of gender identity, (c) how to be intimate with peers, and (d) the discovery of an effective and efficient work or study style.

Individual views of this period of the life cycle (late teenage years) often overlooked or did not even consider the family configuration in how these struggles took place and were resolved. The influences of the family were essentially ignored, as were the effects on the remaining family members when a primary part of their household (i.e., the departing teenager) was removed.

Currently, many mental health professionals treating youngsters preparing to leave home believe that the presenting surface problems of sadness, procrastination, academic anxiety, or relationship difficulties are often related to their changed role in their family system. Teenagers who are no longer physically a part of the family are still responding to the explicit or implicit emotional messages being communicated to them by the other family members; for example, if Sam shares his depressed feelings with his parents upon leaving for college, he may actually be reacting to his old role in the family. Whereas previously he was the mediator in parental arguments, he must now create a distraction or crisis on which the parents can refocus their energy instead of engaging one another in conflict.

Sam's role, desperate but protective, serves a valuable function for the parents. His problems divert their attention away from their original struggles and vulnerabilities in their own relationship.

Pam

Pam, an attractive and creative 18-year-old young woman, was preparing to leave home for an out-of-state college. Her responsible role as the oldest sibling and daughter (she had two younger brothers) was intensified by her mother's sudden death four years before. She viewed herself as "carrying the torch" for her mother by making sure that the rest of the family was taken care of and that her mother's memory was kept alive.

Two months before her graduation, she began to dread her future. She stopped eating for fear of becoming fat and unattractive and became restless, inattentive, and unable to sleep. What had been anticipated as an exuberant celebration of graduation from high school and departure for college was now a time wrought with pain and fear for the family's well-being.

Upon seeing Pam in individual counseling, a therapist quickly determined that Pam's symptoms were not only due to her own insecurity about leaving home and her imagined and real importance to the functioning of the family, but also to the mixed messages she was perceiving from her father and brothers. Whereas they seemed to be happy for her success; in fact, in both behaviors and words, they had implied that their survival as a family was at stake.

Instead of dwelling on Pam's symptoms, which were not life threatening, the therapist decided to include the family in the sessions. This inclusion served to help the family openly acknowledge their varying feelings about Pam's departure and to assure Pam that they would survive. In one of the final family therapy sessions, one brother kidded "We love you Pam, but you're not the only one who knows how to flip pancakes."

Family therapy allowed Pam to remain in charge of the family. She directed and delegated her duties to her brothers and allowed this "passing of the torch" so that she could pursue her interests and dreams and still remain actively involved in family matters. By graduation time, she was on the road to health and recovery and to her college.

Effects on the Family

As the adolescent preparing to leave home is passing through an identifiable developmental stress point, the family, too, is experiencing unique stressors. Professionals who study families acknowledge that the person leaving home is not the only family member passing through a conflictual developmental passage; the entire family must now think of themselves differently, and must adjust their behaviors accordingly. This is especially crucial because of the influence of the interaction between the presenting midlife transitions of the parents and the powerful pressures on the late adolescent's life.

At first glance, it appears that the teenager would be burdened with the most stress and change, because he or she is the one leaving familiar surroundings and roles both at home and in the community. However, considerable stress is also placed on the roles and relationships among the remaining family members. Not only is the teenager faced with a strange and challenging new environment, but the family must rearrange itself so that a new balance will be felt and experienced. In effect, the family and adolescent are experiencing concurrent stresses and changes!

Naturally, the physical separation of the teenager leaving home produces a reduction in the intensity of emotion between child and parents. Although the teenager will certainly be missed by the remaining family members and may miss the previous status of his or her role in the family, both parents and teen acknowledge that it is the appropriate time to separate. With one member physically removed from the family, less direct demands are now placed on the parents as caretakers, and more emphasis is now placed on their roles as husband and wife. No longer is the teenager around to act as a buffer, go between, or supporter of one parent or the other.

Facing Old Problems

For many families, this change may be quite positive; but for all families, it is certain to produce some degree of worry and anxiety. The couple may have to readdress old problems in their relationship that had been submerged during the childrearing years. When the opportunity has come to reconfront these longstanding issues, there may be some understandable reluctance to engage each other in areas of potential conflict.

New Opportunities

The decrease in active attention to the needs of the teenager permits the parents to develop themselves in work or education or to plan extended recreational pursuits. Mothers who may have delayed their own interests now may be freer to give them their full attention. Fathers may find themselves intensifying their work efforts or using the extra time for vacation planning or for socializing.

Bridging Generations

An additional change that occurs during this time period for the parents may be the reinvolvement with their own now-aged parents. As the grandparents are becoming older and more frail, they may welcome or expect extra assistance from their children. This change in roles and status for these parents also carries with it new worries and necessitates further realignments within the family configuration.

Impact on Siblings

Siblings of the departing teen are also impacted by the loss. Their reactions to the changing family may create any number of new dilemmas or conflicts depending on their age, their relationship to the sibling leaving home, or their previous unique role within the family. The leaving of the first or the last child may have especially important influence on the parents and the rest of the family members.

As the family finds itself getting smaller with each child leaving home, the change will have important implications of emotional loss (e.g., a big sister or personal confidant) or even, in some households, significant gains (younger siblings finally getting their own room). Of course, resentment may increase as chores and additional responsibilities may fall to the younger children.

Expression of Mixed Feelings

During this "leaving home" stage of the family life cycle, when change is expected but the outcome unknown, both gains and losses must be anticipated and envisioned. However, for many, this perception of the event of a child leaving home is rarely acknowledged. Families often view this passage as a sign of joyousness and celebration and overlook the fact that it is also a time of emotional loss. They fail to acknowledge this aspect in the passing of their teen's childhood.

Even during such a positive time as a teenager's graduation, there inevitably are certain negative emotions. For instance, if feelings of loss are not identified, they often emerge later in the form of sadness or anger. Or, when the family is resistant to acknowledging the feelings concerning this separation from their son or daughter, it is likely that these feelings will be expressed by the teenager or other family members in the form of psychological distress.

THE DANCE OF RESISTANCE

There are many ways that parents and their departing teenagers interact to resist acknowledging the possible pain of separation. Many of these ways are not always apparent. The following situations describe some possible consequences of avoiding this very important time within the family life cycle.

1. The teenager develops symptoms, such as academic problems or emotional or behavioral difficulties, that require the parents to become actively involved once again in his or her care.

2. One parent becomes overtly depressed, whereas the other hides the sadness through work or other activities to avoid his or her spouse. This leaves the teenager in a position of being forced back into the family unit to help the overtly depressed parent.

3. The parents' arguments or disagreements may intensify causing the teenager to feel the pressure of returning home to his or her previous role as family mediator.

4. One of the other siblings begins to "act out" to ensure that the parents will not confront one another or to mask their own feelings of loss and sadness.

5. The teenager leaving home may experience intense grief over the loss of the hometown sweetheart and may feel the need to return home on weekends. Although the attachment may be genuine, it also allows for a slower transition between home and college. While the girlfriend or boyfriend may be replaceable away from home, what he or she represents is not—coming back home and still being a part of the family. Thus, the possible breakup becomes intensified because there are two losses involved.

6. Even though teenagers leaving home have physically separated from their parents, many stay emotionally involved by taking on interests, whether academically or vocationally, similar to those of their parents. Teenagers who may resist the challenge of finding their own niche in interests, abilities, and vocational direction often stay overly dependent on their parents.

7. Sometimes, unconsciously, the teenager and parents will engage in verbal altercations to create a justification and rationale for leaving. "See? Mom's always yelling at me, so it's for the best that I'm moving away to college."

A FINAL MESSAGE

Leaving home, whether it be for college or work, is a significant event often overlooked by the older teenager and the family. It is natural for both teen and family to experience a range of both joyful and painful emotions. Departing adolescents often struggle with creating their own new social web away from their family. The remaining family must experience some dissonance and alter its dynamics to encompass a changed family constellation. It is important for parents to remember that it is natural to experience mixed emotions concerning a child leaving home. Usually the family will again find a point of stability and comfort.

Changing roles in life bring about considerable uncertainty and produce feelings of guilt and doubt. When teenagers are very close to their families, they usually have taken on very important emotional roles—caretaker of younger siblings, confidant to one or both parents, and so on.

Betrayal of Love

The act of leaving home can be thought of as a betrayal of love, and the feelings that are produced may be unpleasant. Teenagers do not want to see their parents hurt or sad. Some may think that not going away to college is a small sacrifice or payback for the many years their parents spent caring for them. Teenagers, in general, are very protective of their parents, even though they may resort to using immature methods to express their love.

Parents' Ambivalence

Parents, themselves, also feed into this dilemma by providing mixed messages to this "act of abandonment." They may project their own fears and uncertainties of going out into an unprotected world onto their teenager. For them to send their son or daughter to a highly competitive, prestigious school may be unnerving. Their expressed anxieties, whether verbal or nonverbal, heighten the insecurities in their young adult who is already experiencing some self-doubts. This kind of *ambivalent* message also suggests to teenagers that whatever action they take will not totally please their parents. This message is likely to leave teenagers in a quandary—"damned if they do, damned if they don't."

Possible Reactions and What to Say and Do

When situations like this occur, teenagers are susceptible to just giving up, given a hopeless, no-win situation. At this point, parents are likely to notice symptoms of depression in their teens, such as lapses in attention or declining grades. When a son or daughter shows signs of "cold feet," parents should face the possibility that this is a signal that their messages are being confused.

The family at this time needs to examine and discuss openly their genuine feelings about their sense of loss surrounding the act of leaving. Teenagers who are leaving home (or who have already left) need to hear that they are still a part of the family but that everyone can get along without them, though things will certainly be different. Another important time comes when college teens return home for lengthy stays, like summer vacation. The family, as well as the teens, again faces the need to readjust. Parents are now faced with a more independent youngster who may strive to push newer limits and they must review their rules and expectations. The teenager also must confront a somewhat different living situation. It would not be unusual, during the initial return, for the college teen to take to his or her room for a day or two to reflect on these changes and possible reactions from the parents. Hesitant interactions may become the norm, and neither parents nor teenager may understand the strains that are occurring. This can be a potentially difficult time, but, with communication and awareness, this stage is usually transgressed without major upheaval.

Making Uncertainty More Predictable

Change always brings uncertainty; however, parents can make things more predictable by planning for holidays at home or by discussing upcoming visits to the university. Parents should try talking to other parents in similar situations or to upper-class students who are returning home after their first year—not about grades or classes, but about feelings.

Parents need to be very clear with their sons or daughters that they are expected to try their best. This does not mean placing demands on them but rather giving them the message that it is time to put their best foot forward and encouraging them to succeed. Also, parents should let the teens know that they will be interested in hearing about coursework and new experiences—not unlike when they first entered school. Parents should not be upset and feel overwhelmed by their teens' actions: They will be nervous about leaving home and may regress in their behavior; but they are just *acting out* their emotional conflicts and should not need their parents to intervene.

Graduating from high school and leaving home (whether or not, a teenager goes to college) is an important milestone, and acknowledging a teen's mastery of this passage is extremely important. The best thing for a parent to do is to talk about all their feelings during this time. Sometimes, it is essential to bring in an objective facilitator for these important two or three discussions. This can be a mutual friend, a person of the clergy, or, if need be, a mental health professional. Certainly if a teenager is showing severe symptoms of distress that are interfering with school, work, or regular social relations, a call to a mental health professional could be paramount.

THINGS TO REMEMBER

- A teen leaving home produces a myriad of feelings within all members of the family.
- Family roles change when one member leaves. There is a need to readjust the expectations of every family member.
- When teenagers leave home, they may feel insecure about not being the centerpiece in arising family conflicts.
- Oftentimes, the joys of graduation hide the underlying tensions that are due to the impending emotional loss of a family member leaving the home.
- Teenagers must find their own niche away from home in order to pass through their final stages of dependency.
- Leaving home is not an act of betrayal, but it does carry a price. Family members need to be aware of the possible feelings involved in this important developmental and family milestone.

PART TWO

Depression and Suicide in Teenagers

CHAPTER 5

Understanding Clinical Depression

Leeta

Leeta sat slumped in her chair. Disheveled and distracted, she answered questions in a vague and unfocused manner. Only 13 years old, this was her second extended psychiatric hospitalization for depression, suicidal thoughts, and destructive gestures. She was first admitted to the hospital after she slit her wrists with a knife; this time she had become despondent, irritable, and out of control at home. The night before our interview, she had slammed her hand against the wall in an outburst of anger and frustration stating "I can't stand it anymore!"

As in most periods of depression, Leeta's thoughts and reasoning seemed distorted. She expressed a pervasive sense of hopelessness and was certain that she would remain in hospitals for the rest of her life. Fortunately, this was not the case. She was treated with antidepressant medication and became involved in a variety of therapies that focused on accurate reasoning, a more positive self-image, and ways to lessen family turmoil.

One year after this latest hospitalization, Leeta entered our office for a follow-up interview with energy and excitement. "I never thought that I would feel like hanging out with friends and taking dance lessons. I started tap dancing three months ago, and I love it! It's not that I don't get sad once in a while, but it doesn't take over my whole life."

Raquel

Raquel was almost 17. She was a native South American, with cascading brown hair, an olive complexion, well dressed, and noticeably attractive. Although outwardly she appeared very much together, her insides were another story. She felt hurt, sad, and wounded. She could not recall a time in her life when she was happy; "Ever since I can remember, my heart has hurt."

She rolled up her cashmere sweater to display grotesque scars where she had carved designs in her arm with glass. Dispassionately, Raquel recounted several unsuccessful attempts at suicide. She admitted to having used alcohol and drugs since age 9. Raquel related that she never felt "genuine" unless she was "high or stoned." When asked how she fit into her large upper-class family, she identified herself as being the "bad apple" and "black sheep." Raquel had been arrested numerous times for drug possession, truancy, and running away from home. Prior to this admission, various treatment methods were attempted, including placement in a drug treatment program, all to no avail. Her outlook and prognosis matched her expressions of frustration and helplessness.

Henry

Henry was a tall, slender, and handsome 16-year-old who was sad, but very oppositional. Both articulate and interpersonally engaging, he immediately took control of his therapist's office. "Listen, Doc, I'm not exactly sure what you can do for me—many others have tried, but nothing's ever worked! I'll let you know in advance, I'm considered more than a handful, but I'm willing to give you a try . . . it doesn't hurt, right?"

As a boy, Henry had witnessed his parents' double suicide. Later at age 13, he had overdosed on prescription pills. Since that time, he had turned his inward anger onto his outer world. "When I get mad, I feel like I can tear down buildings and shred people to bits. I can't control my behaviors." Often, he acted on these aggressive impulses, and, of course, the results were always self-defeating.

Although obviously very bright, Henry was underachieving academically and had little motivation to do better. "What's the point in trying to do well in school—teachers always screw things up." He mostly blamed others for his misfortunes and always found fault with rules and regulations.

Extremely bitter toward his adoptive parents, he constantly struggled with them. He argued and fought with them at every turn and never let up. Finally, he was placed in a residential treatment center that allowed him the opportunity to work through his longstanding grief. The experience also provided him time to better accept his adoptive family.

DEPRESSION IS MORE THAN "THE BLUES"

Down . . . blue . . . glum . . . out of sorts. How can you tell if your teenager is experiencing the natural ebb and flow of the "wonder" years or if it is something more serious? This is not an easy question. Recognizing and diagnosing teenage depression is not a simple task. But the first steps are to educate yourself, to ask questions, and to listen.

The onset of depression during the teenage years can be gradual or sudden, brief or long-term; and it can be associated with other disorders, such as anxiety, eating disorders, hyperactivity, and substance abuse. Although the incidence of more severe depression in all teenagers is reportedly less than 10 percent, many of the symptoms (e.g., sadness, poor appetite, physical complaints) do exist singularly or together and in varying degrees of intensity. In fact, research has shown that 34 percent of all teens experience depressed moods, even so-called "normal" teens.

The presence of one or two symptoms does not constitute clinical depression. It is when a cluster of depressive symptoms occur together and over time that a more serious disturbance of mood is considered an emotional illness. In recent years, though, instances of both depression and suicide among teenagers has increased dramatically. This alarming relationship has underscored the seriousness of adolescent suicide and the reasons for parents to become aware of the warning signs.

WHAT IS CLINICAL DEPRESSION?

Most people commonly use the term *depression* in casual conversation. "I'm depressed that the Red Sox lost!" or "It depresses me to think of all the food wasted in restaurants." But, what exactly is *clinical depression* and what differentiates it from the common use of the word *depression*?

Clinical depression refers to a condition marked by changes in one's mood and by associated behaviors that range from a mild degree of sadness to intensely experienced feelings of hopelessness and suicidal thoughts. It is sometimes difficult to tell the difference between regular mood swings and more serious emotional problems.

Experiencing a sad mood, feeling the blues, or expressing grief is not the same as suffering from a depressive disorder. Feelings of sadness after an emotional letdown or grieving after the loss of a loved one, though extremely painful, is normal for everyone. Everyday living encompasses a wide range of emotions, including both depressed and elevated states.

The experience of a clinical depression, or what is medically termed a *depressive disorder*, goes beyond normal mood swings. It encompasses an increase in the intensity and length of the everyday expression of emotions and occurs in combination with other physical and psychological symptoms. Depression is best described as an exaggeration of the normal variability in moods. The biggest question then becomes "What is normal?"

Clinical depression often makes people overly tired, evokes intense feelings of inadequacy and worthlessness, and leads to a loss of interest in life. During periods of a clinical depression, symptoms also include (a) marked restlessness, (b) changes in appetite, (c) diminished abilities in concentration, including decision-making skills, and (d) repeated thoughts of death.

Depression looms large and dark; it can be severe and long-lasting, interfering with all aspects of daily life, from school and vocational achievement to social relationships. Depression can change a person's life-style dramatically and may persist for weeks, months, or even years. The pain can be disabling and sometimes even deadly.

RECOGNITION AND DIAGNOSIS

It is often helpful for parents to be aware of how mental health professionals determine clinical depression. In essence, they use the disturbances that are summarized in the list on page 45 to evaluate for clinical depression. The disturbances are usually presented in the form of a checklist of signs and behaviors.

THE "HEAD COLD" OF EMOTIONAL PROBLEMS

Depressive disorders are the most prevalent of mental health problems. They occur across age, sex, socioeconomic class, race, and culture. The

Symptoms of Depression

Individuals who experience at least four of the following symptoms on a daily basis for more than two weeks or whose functioning has become severely impaired by these symptoms would be considered as suffering from a depressive disorder.

☐ Sad, empty, or anxious mood.

☐ Excessive feelings of guilt and worthlessness.

☐ Feelings of helplessness, hopelessness, and pessimism.

☐ Loss of interest in ordinary activities.

☐ Eating and sleeping problems.

☐ Tiredness and decreased energy.

☐ Thoughts of death and suicide.

☐ Increased restlessness and irritability.

☐ Trouble with concentration and remembering things.

estimated economic cost is in the billions of dollars—including lost wages, treatment costs, and loss of productivity. While the human cost cannot be accurately measured, millions of people are affected.

Under the weightiness of depression, families are disrupted, relationships struggle, friendships are strained, and hopes are shattered. Lives, once full of potential and hope, are extinguished by pain. Research suggests that about 15 percent of depressed individuals of all ages commit suicide.

Some individuals experience only a single major depressive episode in a lifetime, whereas others have recurrent episodes. Many individuals, up to one million in the United States, go through cycles of extreme highs and lows. This disturbance, termed *manic-depressive illness* or *bipolar disorder*, is seen in people who have racing thoughts, marked increases in their talking or actions, elated moods for no apparent reason, and grandiose ideas. Less severe forms of depression include what is termed *dysthymic disorder* (a low-grade depressed mood over one to two years) and *adjustment disorders* that are caused by some known stressor and last three to six months. Some people suffer from the blues only during a specific season of the year. This phenomenon is called *seasonal affective disorder*

(SAD) and has been documented in both adult and child-adolescent populations. It has been shown to respond positively to increased daily exposure to light.

A DISTURBANCE OF THE WHOLE PERSON

People who are depressed have their entire being affected. Their feelings, thoughts, attitudes, physical functioning, and behaviors are altered and disrupted. The key observable feature seems to be a marked change in previous activity levels and interests. A woman once considered lively and "together" no longer is; a man who was known for his active dating is no longer interested in romantic relationships; a top high school or college student loses all interest in school and no longer has direction; an elderly person experiences memory loss, confusion, or apathy—all this due to depression.

Not only is there change, but this change lingers for a long time. These changes in functioning are *interactive* in that one kind of symptom can lead to other symptoms and develop into a cycle that is hard to escape without proper treatment. Depression is truly a serious disorder of the mind and body.

Depression can also affect teenagers' entire functioning. This is usually reflected in an overall decline in school performance. They are no longer completing work assignments, and even assignments they complete are done poorly. Because of their lack of interest, general fatigue, and distractions, they cannot prepare for tests, homework is lost or forgotten, and their concentration and attention spans are limited. Depressed teens usually perform at least two letter grades below where they were previously functioning.

A Disturbance of Mood

A disturbance in a person's mood actually defines the *depressive disorder*. Statements such as "I am feeling sad (or down, or blue)" are common. Within the disorder of depression, the person experiences these feelings such that they are exaggerated and different from ordinary feelings. Also, the more intense the feelings, the more painful and distressing they will be to the individual.

Anxiety is another one of the more common feelings experienced during times of depression. Studies report that more than 60 percent of depressed persons feel intense anxiety or other unpleasant bodily states. Other feelings such as guilt, shame, and irritability are also associated with depressed conditions.

A Disturbance of Behavior

There are several behavioral changes that are commonly associated with clinical depression. These include increased restlessness or agitation, reduced activity levels, slowed thoughts and speech, and sometimes excessive crying. These changes become important when they are (a) different from usual behavior, (b) last for a long time, and (c) interrupt one's life.

When teenagers become depressed, they often express their sadness through unusually aggressive or negative actions such as yelling or throwing objects. One mother stated, "Billy started to become really agitated and restless. He would pick on his younger sister, scream at everyone, and even throw things. I had no idea he was depressed. I just thought he was turning out to be a troublemaker!"

Attitude Changes

People who suffer from depression experience feelings of worthlessness, impacting severely on their self-esteem. They often see themselves as inadequate or incomplete and firmly believe that others view them the same way. One 13-year-old girl wrote in her journal, "Absolutely no one in the world likes me—not even my pets."

With a decline in self-concept, teenagers begin to feel that nothing they do ever matters and soon just give up on everything. Worries and fears begin to take over their lives. They start to dread the future and are certain that they are doomed to failure. "Why bother?" and "What's the use?" become frequent anthems. If these thoughts and feelings intensify, thoughts of suicidal attempts may occur.

Disturbances in Thinking

Depressed persons are often preoccupied with inner thoughts and tensions. Complaints about problems in concentration are often expressed. Thinking and speech patterns often slow down, and distorted reasoning is experienced. Pessimistic viewpoints are spoken; the future is no longer promising. They tend to blame themselves for every bad outcome. One ninth-grade teacher described his student like this: "Nathaniel walks around as if the weight of the world is on his shoulders—he feels personally responsible not only for his parents' breakup, but for every argument or quarrel in this classroom!"

Depressed teens experience a gray cloud around them. They may begin to harbor morbid thoughts. Older teens may become preoccupied with the existential worthlessness of living. Their writings and drawings focus on themes of death. This is usually not a time to brag about teens' seriousness or creativity; they may be contemplating much more! It is important to ask them to elaborate on their productions and to talk about what they have been thinking about. Signals of distress come in nonverbal as well as verbal forms.

Physiological and Bodily Changes

About 75 percent of depressed people experience disruptions in eating and/or sleeping. Symptoms of appetite loss and either early morning or frequent awakening are common, as are reports of fatigue. "Tisha drags all the time," reported one father; "she acts if she never gets a good night's sleep."

Along with decreases in energy, there is a subsequent reduction in social contact and a reduction in finding enjoyment in life's experiences. A variety of other complaints, such as nausea and aches and pains, are frequent during these periods. Depressed people sometimes say that they are exhausted or are having a nervous breakdown during severe experiences with depression.

FRUSTRATIONS IN TRYING TO HELP

When depressed, mental and physical feelings of anguish rarely go away. Resistant to cheerful events or good news, these depressed feelings seem to nag day and night. There appears to be no end to the unpleasantness. Some people become so incapacitated that they cannot even pick up the phone to call anyone, including their doctor. If someone tries to help them, they may refuse their assistance because they no longer believe that they can be helped.

Looking back on her first bout of depression, Sylvia, now 23, stated, "Even after I became isolated, occasionally a teacher or a counselor would express concern and offer help. But, at that point, I couldn't see any hope and shrugged off their offers of assistance. Somewhere inside me, I did want help, but I just couldn't reach for it."

As these comments illustrate, concerned adults (including parents) are likely to become very frustrated with depressed teenagers. Although wanting assistance, a depressed teen rarely follows through on advice, refuses direct help, and denies that things can get better. When caught in the throes of sad and self-degrading thoughts, they often feel that they are not worth helping.

UNDERSTANDING THE CAUSES OF DEPRESSION

So now you have some understanding of clinical depression. But like most concerned parents, you want to know the "whys" behind depression and suicidal actions. What causes depression to be such a weighty and painful disorder? Does negative thinking cause a depressed mood, or does a negative mood lead to distorted thoughts? And at what point do thoughts of suicide enter the picture?

For years, disciplines from psychoanalysis and psychology to biology and biochemistry have grappled with the challenge of depression and its possible fatal consequences. Each discipline has attempted to explain the causes and symptoms of clinical depression and has offered treatment alternatives. Each approach has its strengths and sheds light into the darkness of depression; yet no one approach fully explains the complexities of this disorder. Taken together, these approaches offer fairly comprehensive insights into causes, as well as treatment, for depression.

The psychological models of depression (including the psychoanalytic, behavioral, and cognitive schools of thought) have focused their attention on failed early attachment, inability to obtained desired rewards, impaired social relations, and distorted thinking. What has not been made clear is whether these causes produce a depressed episode or are byproducts of a sad existence.

At the same time, considerable gains have been made in viewing depression within the context of a biological framework. From this perspective, diagnostic tests and medications have emerged to counter the negative consequences of depression. These discoveries have focused their attention on the genetic vulnerabilities of individuals who become depressed and the biochemical changes that people experience during periods of depression. With new scientific research and continued updating of psychopharmacological agents and therapeutic strategies, the debilitation of depression may one day be a thing of the past.

Psychoanalytic Models of Depression

Many psychoanalytically oriented descriptions of depression emphasize interruptions in normal development and disturbances in the attachments to parents and other adult caretakers. Depression may arise, for instance, when a loss ("object-loss") is experienced, such as through death or rejection. The removal of this person, who was likely to be loved yet hated for leaving, produces intense feelings that cause a catastrophic diminution of self-esteem leading to a state of depression. Those teenagers who have experienced previous losses are more inclined to overreact emotionally when confronted by a new threat of separation, such as breaking off a dating relationship.

An added focus of attention from analytical thinkers has emphasized later adolescence as *the* critical period for handling these stronger feelings of powerlessness. The process of separation (from parents) and individuation (developing one's own individual characteristics) normally occurs during adolescence and leads to a sense of competency. Teenagers who have not been able to successfully find their own niche are left behind with a profound feeling of failure that can lead to excessive eruptions in their reactions to stress. To reduce the intensity of these feelings and urges, these teenagers may turn to alcohol and drugs as a method of self-medication. However, this ultimately has the potential for lowering the control of their impulses and may lead them to act out their personal misery.

Although psychoanalytic models had an early impact on the study of depression, they did not generate much empirical research, nor were they successful in developing specific treatment procedures. The most influential approaches to depression are those that have demonstrated some success in treatment. These approaches fall into two general categories: the behavioral models and cognitive models of depression.

A Behaviorist Understanding of Depression

During the 1960s and early 1970s, behavioral viewpoints in psychology flourished. In general, the principles of learning theory (i.e., how the environment influences behavior) were used predominantly to explain both normal and abnormal behavior. Behaviorists viewed depression as a consequence of no longer receiving adequate or sufficient reinforcement. This could be caused by (a) environmental changes, (b) the loss of the person who provided rewards and pleasure, or (c) the individual's inability to secure positive reinforcement. For the teenager susceptible to depression, a reduction in the amount of available rewards might be due to (a) losing a parent through death, separation, or divorce; (b) breaking off an interpersonal relationship; (c) exclusion from a sports team or other school-related organization; or (d) being fearful or shy (which would limit participation in social events, such as teen dances or dating).

Loss of Rewards

Because the potential for reward is no longer available or has been reduced substantially, the behaviors that were being maintained by these rewards are now being lowered, leading to even fewer pleasurable interactions. The teenager ultimately becomes more passive, lessening his or her own expectations and actions, leading to poor self-esteem and depression.

Behaviorists also suggest a kind of feedback loop that serves to keep the depressive cycle intact. If the depression is created by the lack of obtainable rewards, for instance, the symptoms may continue because the person may gain sympathy for his or her sad mood, producing the attention and concern that is actually desired. However, the sympathy is usually short-lived, because even the most caring people begin to avoid the depressed person. This causes a reduction in attention, and the person becomes more and more depressed.

Lack of Social Skills

An added viewpoint from a behaviorist perspective suggested that a key element in depression is a lack of social skills. These deficits in interpersonal functioning include characteristics such as (a) feeling uncomfortable during social interchanges, (b) seldom receiving a positive response from others, and (c) being especially sensitive to perceived interpersonal slights. Because behaviorists contend that a decrease in being rewarded for favorable behavior will ultimately result in a sad mood and lead to self-blame, persons with few social skills would be highly susceptible to depression due to their already low level of obtaining reinforcement.

The learning of social competencies is especially important for teenagers whose major tasks through these years (e.g., becoming independent, forming meaningful relationships, increasing a sense of competence) are highly dependent on discovering effective communication styles and broadening their interpersonal experiences. For teenagers, a lack of these skills would most assuredly result in ostracism from others, personal isolation, and an impaired self-concept.

Learned Helplessness

Another recent behaviorist model—the learned helplessness theory of depression—addressed the learning side of motivation and how it could impact on mood.

Animal and human experiments by Martin Seligman and his colleagues at the University of Pennsylvania were able to demonstrate how uncontrollable or unwarranted punishment and failure would lead to deficits in responding, learning, and the expression of emotion. In essence, both animals and humans could "learn" to become helpless. This guiding principle could help explain many of the frustrating behaviors seen in learning-disabled children, in institutionalized adults, and in populations of elderly people in whom failure, negative feedback, or loss would be present no matter the effort involved in overcoming the perceived problems.

Teenagers undoubtedly have less experience than adults with negative life events (e.g., death or divorce) that are out of their control. Additionally, their spurts of physical growth and uneven skill development may leave them feeling that things are truly beyond their control and that events have no bearing on their efforts. They are likely then to become passive and distressed and to lose confidence in their abilities, with the result being that they appear and act helpless and dependent.

Cognitive Models of Depression

Theorists and practitioners who espouse cognitive explanations of depression assume that (a) how people view themselves and their world will determine how they will feel and act and (b) thoughts and feelings are interrelated (i.e., one cannot feel down or blue without also having upsetting thoughts). Persons who believe that they must be successful at all times, for example, may feel deeply depressed or anxious when faced with failure. Conversely, bad feelings about a failure may initiate distorted or irrational thinking ("I'll never succeed again").

Distortions in Thinking

According to these cognitive explanations, when a person becomes clinically depressed, a bias of extreme negativism prevails; that is, he or she becomes preoccupied with degrading views toward (a) the self (e.g., "I am no good"), (b) the world (e.g., "They are no good," "It's too hard"), and (c) the future (e.g., "It is always going to be this way"). This distorted thinking (these cognitions) may or may not be at the root of the depression and suicide, but it maintains feelings of helplessness and undermine one's mood and energy level.

When experiencing cognitive distortions during periods of depression, one (a) may become easily frustrated, interpreting small setbacks as monumental; (b) may feel slighted by otherwise harmless statements; and (c) may frequently devalue oneself by never acknowledging strengths and often deflecting compliments. Interpretations of actual events during depressed times are rarely accurate and are consistently negative and self-critical.

Cognitive theorists emphasize that the observable symptoms of depression can best be understood within these distortions in thinking. Depressed individuals often misinterpret their situations and begin to feel defeated, deprived, or deserted. As a consequence, they view themselves as impotent in most aspects of their lives. They become more likely to make hurtful self-statements when faced with continued failure or rejection (i.e., "I must be at fault"). Next, they begin to generalize these faulty conclusions to other situations and to no longer see any hope of gaining satisfaction. These negative beliefs then become the root for maintaining and increasing their depressive symptoms and suicidal thoughts.

Pessimistic Outlooks

Studies have shown that teenagers also develop a pessimistic thinking pattern when depressed. They begin to see themselves as inadequate and less able than their peers. Depressed teens no longer perceive themselves as able to cope with even minor problems. They no longer can set obtainable goals. Any demands made on them seem overwhelming. Small obstacles appear insurmountable. They are convinced that there is no end to their problems.

Hopeless Feelings

Depressed teenagers also feel powerless to alter the downward emotional cycle in which they find themselves. Feelings of shame and guilt are commonplace. These negative feelings are likely to lead to further frustrations and to undermine their confidence and initiative. More often than not, they feel that no one can help them out of their misery. They become isolated and feel alone, even in the presence of family or friends. Their feelings are narrowed by an everpresent dim and pessimistic outlook and lead to feelings of hopelessness.

Narrowed Thinking

Along with these feelings are thoughts that have become overly constricted. No longer do depressed teenagers have the ability to investigate and consider options to solve problems or to overcome adversity. Dichotomous, or all-or-nothing, thinking dominates their reasoning. A search for solutions has to be 100 percent effective, or else total failure is expected.

Suicide: The Only Option

Unfortunately, suicide is often considered a viable option when chosen solutions are not perfect. The stress that may occur from even small setbacks becomes too overwhelming to consider. Teenagers at this point cannot tolerate the pain of trying and failing. This type of tunnel vision and arbitrary logic can handle only one piece of information: that the "only" solution is suicide and that the "only" method is killing oneself. Nothing else, in this teen's view, can end the pain.

Typical Teen Distortions

Teenagers are experts at such typical distortions as *overgeneralizing* from a single experience ("I failed to get a date—no one will ever go out with me!") or *catastrophizing* ("My world is falling apart!"). Although these faulty assumptions are commonly heard among many teenagers, they become more pronounced during times of depression. They also make teenagers more susceptible to maintaining these types of distorted perceptions. Subsequently, their moods change rapidly and they are more likely to act out these thoughts and feelings in a conflictual manner. Once inside this cycle of distorted conclusions about interpersonal incidents (e.g., blaming oneself after a rejection from peers), it is hard to step out of this downward spiral without assistance.

Chain Effects of Negative Thinking

These distortions in perceptions and reasoning lead to a vicious cycle of self-defeating thoughts, negative feelings, and low motivation. The negative view of themselves and the gloomy outlook for their world and their future become pervasive and severely impair their performance at home and school. The chain effects lead to more perceived failure and negative feedback from others, which keep them isolated and unable to change. The results of all this faulty logic are teenagers who withdraw from others and lack initiative.

Biological Models of Depression

Biological models of depression can be divided into two main categories: (a) those that focus on the biochemical correlates of depression and (b) those that emphasize the role of genetic factors.

Actions of Neurotransmitters

Much of the biochemical research has centered on the actions of neurotransmitters, which are natural chemicals that allow communication among brain cells. Evidence indicates, for instance, that depressed people have abnormalities in their metabolism of neurotransmitters that can be counteracted through the use of antidepressant medication. However, there is no certainty about whether the abnormalities are a primary cause of the depression or a secondary symptom.

Persons who are suffering from depression-related disorders have been found to have (a) a deficit of neurotransmitters, which may lead to depression; (b) an excess of neurotransmitters during manic episodes; or (c) an imbalance of neurotransmitters.

Two such neurotransmitters that have been researched extensively are serotonin and norepinephrine. An imbalance of serotonin can produce such common depressive symptoms as sleep irregularities, irritability, and increased anxiety. Similarly, when an inadequate amount of norepinephrine (which regulates alertness and arousal) is being produced, fatigue and a sad mood are likely to result.

Imbalance of Other Bodily Chemicals

Other bodily chemicals may be out of balance during times of depression. One such chemical is cortisol, a hormone that is produced in response to extremely cold temperatures or excessive displays of emotions (e.g., rage or fear). On average, the level of cortisol in the bloodstream peaks in the morning and decreases as the day continues. However, when someone is depressed, the level remains constant throughout the day. A blood test—the Dexamethasone Suppression Test (DST)—has been developed to demonstrate this increase in cortisol level in depressed individuals. This physiological test is one more diagnostic instrument that can be used to confirm whether someone is clinically depressed.

Investigations into neuroendocrine abnormalities have also been a source for describing biochemical explanations of depression. It is believed that many depressive symptoms (e.g., lack of energy, blue mood) allude to difficulties in the regulation of the hypothalamus. Additionally, the neurotransmitters that normally monitor the agents that mediate pituitary and other hormonal activity (e.g., acetylcholine) have been shown to be imbalanced during periods of depression.

The Role of Genetics

The role of genetics in depression has been expanded primarily through studies of twins and adoptees. Research indicates an average concordance rate of 76 percent for mood disorders in monzygotic (identical) twins versus a rate of 19 percent for dizygotic (fraternal) twins. Similarly, adoption studies have demonstrated a higher incidence of depression in adoptees whose biological parents suffered from an affective disturbance.

Scientific discoveries during the past two decades have also focused attention on the genetic influences that contribute to depression. One prime example is that researchers have attempted to pinpoint genetic markers that leave certain individuals susceptible to manic-depressive illness. Though a specific gene has not been found, the existence of these genetic markers brings researchers closer to this conclusion.

The consideration of genetic markers suggests more support for earlier studies reporting familial links in depressive illness; for instance, close relatives of individuals suffering from major depression are more susceptible to depressive symptoms than nonrelatives.

Evidence provided from studies of twins has shown that if one twin becomes depressed, the other has a 70 percent chance of also experiencing the various symptoms of depression. These rates have also been demonstrated in studies on adopted children. While adoptive families are at little risk of transmitting their symptoms, adoptive children have been shown to be three times more likely to become depressed if their biological relatives experienced periods of depression.

As evidence emerges from genetic studies, other investigators are exploring questions relating genetic markers to family histories, to depression treatment response, and to subtype classifications of depression. Conversely, there has been a renewed emphasis on exploring biological markers in those people who have been determined to be at risk for suicide because of family history, regardless of whether they are manifesting symptoms.

The Future

Many issues remain in trying to describe the symptoms, course, and treatment of teenage depression. With the increased activity of exploring the biochemical and genetic bases of depression, more insights will certainly be forthcoming during the next decade and next century that will help to explain both the transmission and the mechanism of action during times of depression.

THINGS TO REMEMBER

- Clinical depression is more than just the normal ups and downs of successes and failures.
- Depression in adolescence is often related to many problems during this time period; whether depression is the primary cause of these problems or whether other factors cause depression remains to be clarified.
- Depression impacts one's entire being, resulting in disturbance of mood, behavior, attitude, thinking and in physiological and bodily changes.
- It is important to be aware of the signs and symptoms for which mental health professionals look for in determining clinical depression.
- Suicidal thoughts and suicide attempts are among the most serious risks of depression.
- There are many theories and models of depression; taken together they offer much information about the causes and courses of this common emotional problem.
- Most of the current thinking about depression stems from the success of treatment programs that use medication and cognitive-behavioral therapy approaches.
- Depression results from a combination of factors—biological vulnerability, upbringing, and social experiences—thus making treatment quite challenging.

CHAPTER 6

Is Your Teenager Depressed?

Gary

Gary had longstanding problems of oppositionality, poor impulse control, and identity struggles. Now 15, he had been in outpatient therapy since age 8, when he was diagnosed with hyperactivity. He had also been hospitalized for two brief periods due to excesses in his behavior that led to theft and volatility in his home. His school behavior and performance had now taken a turn for the worse, and there was suspicion of alcohol abuse. It was determined that he may have been suffering from a depressive disorder. With this point of view and much therapeutic input through individual and family therapy, he began to show improvement.

Joan

Joan, 16 years old, had been expressing an intolerable level of anger and defiance in her home. Additionally, her school performance had been deteriorating and her friendships strained. Her continued difficulties led to a consideration of removing her from home. In previous years, attempts at outpatient therapy and special school programs only provided minimal progress as she showed little motivation to change. After a thorough evaluation, it was determined that her underlying depression had never been treated. Plans were discussed for a more intensive treatment strategy that included a brief hospitalization, frequent outpatient therapy, and placement on antidepressant medication.

Andy

Andy had been hospitalized after consuming an overdose of pills he had obtained from his parents' medicine cabinet. At 16 years old, Andy had always been a good student and no problem to his parents and teachers. However, he had always viewed himself as shy and anxious and never a part of the more popular crowd at school. He seldom took social risks and never had the opportunity to practice the skills required to feel comfortable around others. This left him feeling lonely, anxious, and alienated. He concluded that he did not have anything of interest to offer anyone. Inside, Andy was suffering, but he never revealed his immense insecurities or his fears to others.

After struggling to ask someone out for an important dance and being rejected, Andy felt discouraged and defeated. He was sure that his life would never change and that he would always feel frustrated and pained. Suicide seemed the only way to relieve his inner stress and to show everyone that he was really suffering.

After he was hospitalized, Andy was startled to find that others shared similar thoughts and feelings. He discovered that his peers were as negative toward themselves as he had become. Statements such as "I am too short" (or ugly or stupid or lazy) were common among most of the teenagers on the unit. Everyone seemed willing to accept fault with themselves for every setback or complication in their lives.

This was a breakthrough for Andy who attributed everything wrong in life to his own shortcomings. With professional assistance that offered him alternatives to his misperceptions, he was able to see himself in more positive terms and to view his world as more inviting. Soon, he was able to reenter his home and school and to begin forming meaningful relationships with his peers.

DISGUISES OF THE TEENAGE YEARS

Although there are many teenagers who have experienced the same kinds of problems as Gary, Joan, and Andy, most teenagers' problems are not as dramatic; yet they may be experiencing many feelings of depression that are undermining their growth and potential. They may be oversleeping in the mornings to avoid stressful situations; their concentration and subsequently their school grades may be declining; previous interests may no longer motivate them; or they seem especially moody. Something is going on, and the parents (and they) may be confused by these new feelings and behaviors. What really is going on? Is it truly a cause for alarm and a rush to therapy?

Even after reading the previous chapter and understanding the course and causes of clinical depression, it may still not be enough to truly understand the behavior of adolescents. Depression in teenagers often goes unrecognized or is written off as merely a passing youthful phase. Even within the professional community, the existence of adolescent depression has remained controversial, although recent evidence tends to confirm its authenticity.

Teenagers are not adults. It is difficult to define a particular disorder of adults and translate it into terms that make sense for a younger age group. Teenagers often try actively to cover up their feelings because of embarrassment and negative feedback from others or from their own denial. They wear a variety of self-made masks that effectively conceal their inner stress and turmoil. Only by removing these masks can parents view their teenagers in a different light.

It is also common for depression in teenagers to co-exist with other psychiatric conditions, such as anxiety, drug abuse, and eating disorders. The most common co-morbid disturbances during the teen years tend to be anxiety and conduct disorders (characterized by defiance and unlawful conduct). With female adolescents, there is a high correlation between eating disorders and depression. Substance abuse also occurs very frequently with depression. There is no definitive answer about whether depression causes these other disorders or vice/versa. When these disorders do occur together, it makes treatment more difficult and makes the problems more difficult to overcome.

Since the period of adolescence is defined by rapid physical and emotional change, clinical depression in the young is often overlooked. This oversight is understandable; the only real difference between "normal" ups and downs and clinical depression is the duration and intensity of the expressed symptoms. In the past, the general myth was that most adolescents experience troubled times. Recent research suggests otherwise, because most teens traverse this period relatively smoothly. Those teens who are struggling may very well require professional intervention.

THE PARENTS' DECISIONS

Parents know their children better than any other person. So parents must make a judgment whether their sons or daughters are truly experiencing more than the usual mood swings. A good barometer is to compare them to other neighborhood children. Parents should decide if their teens are truly acting up or showing more signs of sadness or anger than other children and if they (the parents) are really worried that this will not pass.

Parents must be able to assess their own unique family situation and to see whether the actions of their teenager are totally disrupting the family organization. If doubts persist, they should not hesitate to seek advice from school counselors or clergy, or to call directly for professional mental health assistance.

The teen years are a valuable time for learning. Any severe interruption can create lags in development, thus delaying progress toward a full and productive adulthood. Why not get them the necessary help? The decision to seek treatment is certainly influenced by many factors, such as perceived need, insurance, belief in therapy, and so on; but sometimes it is better to try than to just sit back and hope for the best.

TEENS STRIVING FOR FREEDOM

Teenagers do not want to feel dependent on their parents or relatives. Because of this age-appropriate attitude, parents are unlikely to hear their teenager request help to overcome their sad feelings. For many teenagers, this action would be hypocritical. After all, they are desperately trying to escape from feeling like they need their parents all the time.

Teenagers want to flex their muscles of maturity and self-reliance. Instead of recognizing that they may actually require some assistance, depressed teens tend to scoff at advice from adults and to blame others for their misery. A depressed teen is likely to be overheard saying things like "If only she would just mind her own business" or "Stay away from my problems."

In addition to blaming others, teenagers are usually not savvy enough to recognize and diagnose their own depression. Teenagers do not have enough valuable life experiences. Teenagers are action-oriented, and they usually hide depressed feelings under statements like, "I'm bored." They even scoff at direct questioning of depression, responding instead with statements like, "Wouldn't you be bored if you had to stay in school all day?" It is not school per se, but the depression that colors their views. What they fail to realize is that when one is depressed, everything can seem boring.

Teenagers do not want to experience anxiety or pain. They run away from it as fast as they feel it coming. Desperately, they seek escape avenues and look for momentary thrills without contemplating the broader picture. The teenage years are for heightened experimentation. Often, this thrill seeking can lead to alcohol and drug use and to unwanted or ill-prepared sexual encounters. The result can only maintain the hard and troubling times.

A FAMILY PROBLEM

For many depressed teenagers, their symptoms of depression are often a reflection of what is happening in the family. For example, if teenagers try to express sad feelings and only receive criticism, denial, or rejection from adults, they may become disruptive in order to express their anger at parents who are ignoring their true feelings.

Another important consideration is whether the teenager's depression is related to the feelings of others in the family. When parents are struggling over marital or career problems, teens may feel the tension created by these conflicts and try to distract their parents by redirecting the attention to themselves. One powerful option that teenagers possess if they sense their family situation getting strained is to blatantly express severe depressive or suicidal feelings; they do this so the parents can clearly see that they are still needed in their primary role as parents.

Teenagers use these symptoms to ensure that their parents will not become preoccupied in their own misery and that the parents will continue to exert their energy and focus on them, the teens. This is a very protective role for teenagers who may be trying to help their parents in the only way they know how.

THE TOTAL PICTURE

Adolescent depression is more than just a mood or an isolated problem. The sadness does not occur alone. It is associated with combinations of other symptoms to form a broader picture. The clinical disorder of depression has a specific form with a specifiable course. However, since the experience of sad feelings is familiar to most everyone and is normal when dealing with life stress, family members and friends are likely to minimize the severity of symptoms in a depressed teenager.

Adults, even caring ones, are just not likely to attribute clinical depression to teenagers, even though signs of apathy or restlessness may be observed. Parents tend to describe their problem teenager as lazy or manipulative rather than as depressed. "There is nothing wrong with him" or "He's not sick (or crazy), he's just demanding," parents commonly say to doctors and counselors. Parents just seem to have a natural inclination toward ascribing character traits to children rather than toward thinking in terms of an emotional disturbance or illness.

Parents should not expect their teenagers to confirm their suspicions and fears. Teenagers themselves misattribute their own symptoms; they are more likely to blame their problems on parents, siblings, or teachers than to think that they are depressed. All these misperceptions usually result in power struggles, while the truer picture regarding the teenager's illness remains neglected. Often, it takes a more objective person, such as a mental health professional, to establish that the changes taking place in the teenager's mood, behavior, thoughts, and body are of an intensity and persistence to justify treatment for depression.

COMMON QUESTIONS AND ANSWERS

The following section is an attempt to summarize the warning signs of teenage depression through common questions that are often asked of mental health professionals in their practices and the answers they are likely to give. The questions and answers focus on the many problems that are presented to mental health professionals and are important concerns to the families being affected.

Obtaining an Accurate Diagnosis

"I've heard all kinds of opinions about my son's condition, and he has been labeled all kinds of things. Now you are saying that depression can be causing many of his problems. Who and what am I to believe? It seems as though each doctor and educational authority has a different opinion. Also, the labels and diagnoses seem to change over time."

You are not alone in wondering what to believe about your son's condition—many parents share your bafflement. Diagnosing an emotional disturbance has always been somewhat subjective and controversial within the health and mental health fields. The latest revised editions of the *Diagnostic and Statistical Manual of Mental Disorders* (DSM-III-R and DSM-IV) (American Psychiatric Association, 1987, 1994), the "bible" used for diagnosing mental illness, have attempted to become more objective in defining the various classifications of disturbance but, unfortunately, still pay little attention to child and adolescent issues. The relative invisibility of this age group is a reflection of both society's and professionals' lack of appropriate concern. The issue of a clear diagnosis for adolescent depression seems even more confusing to the general public.

Part of your confusion about your son's diagnosis stems from the fact that depression in children and adolescents, like many of the disorders only attributable to adult dysfunction, has never been taken seriously until very recently. Theorists, researchers, and clinicians were cautious to place serious labels on still maturing youth whose feelings and problematic behaviors often do pass with time and whose personalities are adaptive to change.

Acknowledging that your child could be clinically depressed is painful. Symptoms of depression seen in adolescents have always been attributed to temporary stress, behavior problems, or personality conflicts. However, it is now seen that many youth suffer quietly and without relief. These are the ones that have heretofore been labeled as shy, lazy, or bad; and they, like any other sufferer, deserve treatment. Your son has assuredly been labeled with some of these names—and maybe a myriad of other ones as well.

During the past decade, there has been a growing consensus among professionals that depression and other related emotional disturbances do indeed affect children and adolescents and cause serious repercussions. Depressive symptoms do distort one's thinking and reactions. These changes lead to a negative and self-defeating cycle that can interfere with present functioning and new learning. Once in a depressed state, teenagers like your son are also likely to irritate and offend adults and peers. They then receive punitive and critical feedback that will likely maintain the depression and further impair their already vulnerable self-esteem.

In addition, this newer view of depression recognizes that symptoms of depression do often co-occur with other disorders. Children who have learning disabilities, for example, may begin to act out their frustrations over their inability to solve problems that appear easy to others. Their disruptive reactions will likely elicit negative feedback from adults and peers. Without positive support and accurate feedback from others, they never gain the opportunity to learn the skills to overcome their difficulties. They begin to feel helpless about ever being able to accomplish or master anything, and they feel sad and hopeless about things ever improving for them. Their actions, if extremely disruptive, may lead to a diagnosis of conduct disorder when, in fact, their behaviors are merely reflecting an underlying depressive disorder.

Since teenagers are still in school, they also come under a different system for documenting and labeling their problems or disorders. Your son may very well have undergone extensive testing in school. However, educational codes are *not* clinical diagnoses. They are used for classroom placement and educational resource help and not for therapeutic intervention. This system has clouded diagnostic issues even further and often creates more confusion for parents. A teenager who is considered by educational standards as "socially and emotionally disturbed," for example, will be designated by the school system for special placement and will receive services that may include counseling. However, the label gives no indication as to the exact nature or the extent of the problem or to other noneducational ways to intervene, which is the primary purpose of a diagnostic system.

Diagnosing a problem, such as your son's, is a process that clearly describes an individual's condition in order to select the most appropriate method for treatment. It is a system to translate symptoms into a coherent picture so that health and mental health professionals can work toward resolving the problem. Certainly, you would not want a surgeon to remove your child's lung if he were diagnosed as having a stomach ailment. Similarly you do not want your depressed teenager treated with a therapeutic approach or a particular medication that is not meant for depression.

Symptoms, feelings, and behaviors are all so very interrelated that it makes trying to clearly define a specific disorder very confusing. That is one reason why multiple diagnoses are encouraged by the newest revisions of the DSM. Yet even this attempt to give credit to all displayed symptoms sometimes gives parents conflicting messages. And if you are receiving conflicting messages, you can be sure your teenager is experiencing confusion also. Your son may be as ready to pull his hair out as you are!

If you have any doubts about your child's diagnosis or treatment plan that cannot be explained clearly by the treating professional, it is always best to seek a second or even a third opinion. Your questioning should be specific and plentiful until you become satisfied that the diagnosis is accurate and the treatment is best for your teen. This is especially important when expensive evaluations are ordered or medications are being prescribed. Your physician or therapist will expect you to supply as much pertinent information as you can, so you should not hesitate to ask as many questions as necessary and expect to receive genuine answers and impressions before deciding upon your teenager's condition.

Unfortunately emotional problems are not as clear-cut as physical ones, but a clear, concise explanation of how someone derived the diagnosis and the planned treatment approach should be demanded. And through this give-and-take process, you, and other parents, can expect to become educated consumers, which is so very important when it comes to a child's mental health and how it may impact on the family. Learning what to expect goes a long way in gaining some control during a very stressful period.

Hyperactivity and Depression

"Our son Marvin, who is 12, was diagnosed as hyperactive many years ago and, after several years of unsuccessful therapies, was successfully treated with Ritalin. Now he is approaching his teen years, and we are not sure what to expect. We've heard some people say that kids outgrow hyperactivity. Is this true? What should we look out for?"

Children, like Marvin, who are truly hyperactive or who have what is currently termed attention-deficit hyperactivity disorder (ADHD) have started out in life with a problematic condition. Up to the age of 12, this condition has resulted in impulsive behaviors, a lack of frustration tolerance, and an inability to concentrate and complete tasks. As a result, these children are generally viewed as disruptive in school and surely have received substantial negative feedback for their hard-to-manage behaviors. Those successfully treated with medication and other therapies can regain some confidence after a rocky start to their schooling.

As Marvin grows into his teenage years, the symptoms displayed by his attention deficits do not magically disappear. However, many teens—and Marvin may be one of them—learn compensatory strategies to overcome their weaknesses. As they become older and more independent, they discover more avenues to channel their excess energy. They may also find personal strengths to utilize their abilities in a more productive manner and may have somewhat better control of their expressed emotions. All of these added personal skills may at least reduce some of their extreme behaviors.

Residual effects of the disorder remain, however. In addition, the adolescent years bring on different demands that continue to negatively affect the type of interpersonal feedback that teens might receive, which could further damage their already vulnerable self-esteem. Many hyperactive children never had the opportunity to practice social skills and are now confronted with the more sophisticated social demands of being a teenager. This may likely lead to feelings of embarrassment, humiliation, and personal failure.

Having impaired social relations throughout high school may mean feelings of isolation, rejection, and a sense of alienation. With the onset of adolescence and its preoccupation with self and comparison to others, hyperactive children may be more sensitive to their differences and, feeling more alone, may become susceptible to bouts of depression.

In school, hyperactive children may still experience problems in attending to the teacher, completing assignments, or organizing their work. These difficulties, although now more subtle, will still be a reminder of past failures and may lead to moodiness, anger, and irritability. Hyperactive children may still be acting out their feelings, but now they may choose alcohol or drug usage, or become engaged in delinquent activities, to express their inner sense of personal ineffectiveness.

Like any childhood illness that impairs normal functioning, hyperactivity can become a long-term struggle. It is important to recognize that a child who has not had a successful elementary school experience will probably continue to experience problems, although these will likely be expressed in a different manner. With the help of Ritalin, your son was able to experience some successes, and this will have boosted his confidence.

Every child needs plenty of support and encouragement when entering adolescence, especially those vulnerable children who may have been suffering from ADHD. They continue to need help and can benefit from counseling, especially from small group experiences where social skills can be gained.

Hyperactive children continue to hurt inside. Therefore, obtaining professional assistance at this important stage in their life is crucial to ensure further awareness of their problem and to help them deal more effectively with the coming years.

Hiding Behind Their Anger

"Our son seems so out of control. I know he must be hurting inside, but he gets so frustrated and angry when he can't get his point across. He has been in many fights and suspended from school more than once. We are afraid to approach him because of his anger and usually just let him go his own way. We have tried outpatient therapy before, but he was too resistant and made such a fuss that we just thought our money was being wasted. We know he will soon get in trouble with the law if he doesn't change or if we don't do something drastic. Should we contact the juvenile authorities for help, or try to get him hospitalized for a short while?"

You are correct in assuming that your son is hurting and is probably very frustrated himself. It also sounds like he has been able to alienate many others who may have attempted to reach out to him. This is always a tough scenario.

All the strategies he has used before to gain success, either academically or socially, have failed him. He probably gives up easily on most things and has no expectations of himself or others. He has closed off many avenues of expression and prefers to act out his frustrations through being defensive or irritable and sometimes aggressive. All these actions most likely turn others off and leave him feeling lonely; at the same time, he probably thinks that no one cares about him. In turn, since he feels unloved, he must treat others in the same manner and may blame them for his plight and misfortune.

It sounds like your son has always had similar problems that are either due to early learning problems or emotional limitations that have inhibited his ability to progress along with his peers. He is stuck at an earlier stage in development, but now people are expecting more of him because of his age and size. This can cause incredible stress for your son, stress that he may cope with through fighting or arguing.

Teenagers like your son can be helped, but it usually takes a team effort involving many people. You may want to have more meetings with his teachers to emphasize your concerns (although I am sure that you have spent more days at school than your son has by now) and to pursue more ideas. Although your initial attempt at outpatient therapy may not have worked, you should not give up that easily. I would encourage you to try again, but make sure the person you go to specializes in difficult and troubled youth.

Within this context, it is always helpful to find clinicians that work with groups of teens because peer messages can often be more powerful than messages from adults.

Calling on juvenile authorities can be beneficial because many of their workers are eager to help troubled youth. Some newer programs even provide workers to visit homes on a daily basis to see teenagers. They can usually find alternative sources of recreation or jobs that could channel a teenager's energy more appropriately and give him or her a source of rewards and personal satisfaction for accomplishment. Sometimes, just the threat of involving the juvenile workers can get a youth's attention; but threats rarely work.

Finally, all intervention should start with a comprehensive diagnosis. Your pediatrician or family doctor could be your first stop for ruling out various problems. After this, psychological and educational evaluations can provide valuable information to better understand your son's strengths and weaknesses and offer direction in any planned intervention. Often, this can be gained through your school, local mental health center, or the psychiatry department within a hospital.

If your son becomes extremely oppositional to these plans, an extended evaluation in a hospital is one alternative. Although extreme, it does allow for a more thorough observation period and the opportunity for information to be gathered from a number of sources. Also, if a trial of medication is warranted, it can be closely monitored in the hospital, and feedback can be given in a safe environment.

One alternative to hospitalization is day treatment. In these partial hospitalization programs, the youth remains for the entire day but returns home each night. It is less expensive than 24-hour care and provides the opportunity for most interventions to be tried. This option is available if the youth is not a clear danger to himself or herself or others.

At this time, it seems that you and your family need support. There are many organizations for parents who are having difficulties with their troubled teens. You may want to call on your local Mental Health Association to solicit available options (also, the Appendix in the back of this book describes many nationwide organizations that can provide information). Often teachers, your clergy, or the local hospital or university have names and phone numbers to call.

Remember, parenting a teenager is possibly the most difficult time for anyone. Adding complications such as school problems, emotional outbursts, or legal difficulties only increase the family stress. There are many people who want to help, and you should be able to find a helpful ear—but you must act and be receptive to many new ideas.

Drugs and Teenage Depression

"We think our 15-year-old son is doing drugs; but his sudden change in behavior and interests may be due to symptoms of depression. How can we be sure? We don't want to accuse him of doing drugs if he's depressed instead."

It is difficult to tell whether a person is depressed because of a mood disturbance, or is experiencing a change in mood and behavior that has been induced by drugs. Someone who is taking drugs may become irritable and may show weight gain or loss, irregular sleeping patterns, change of work and study habits, or a loss of interest in previously enjoyed activities. For the parent who wants to be supportive and encouraging, this becomes quite a dilemma. Any confrontation will likely create more tension, but denying that there is a problem will only make matters worse.

Teenagers do not want to be intruded upon; but as a parent, you must. This is never an easy matter. Reach out to neighbors, friends, teachers, and others who know your son to obtain confirmation that something is indeed different about him. Tell them that you are concerned because you have noticed these changes and are asking them about their views. Also, it is okay to look through your son's room for drugs (this does not mean prying into private papers or other personal possessions). It is still your house and privacy counts only in an environment of trust.

When you have gathered some facts to either relieve yourself that your son is not involved in drugs or have discovered that your son is taking drugs, it is time to express some level of concern so that he can begin finding alternatives to his problems. If this cannot be done on a parent-to-child basis, maybe you can enlist the aid of relatives. If this only alienates your son more, you may want to consider turning to professional help.

It is important to view depression or drug use as a problem that is impacting on the whole family and not only on your son. By including the entire family, it increases the message of love and concern and brings the problems out in the open so that they can be discussed.

If your son refuses this kind of approach on an outpatient basis or is exhibiting severe symptoms that may lead to behaviors dangerous to himself or others, it is best to access a nearby hospital that can offer a safe environment in which to explore all options. If drugs are the problem, it would be best to also solicit help from parent support groups in your community. These can be accessed through your school counselor, clergy, or family doctor. The main thing to do is act—your teenage son's life is passing him by if his emotional or drug problems are not being treated.

WHAT PARENTS CAN DO

In times of distress, conflict, or crisis, even the best of relationships can suffer. These troubled times present the need for family, friends, and teachers to learn new ways of listening to each other. If you see that your teen is depressed, there is much you can do to help. Begin by making it clear that you are concerned and willing to listen. Next, listen to feelings in a genuine and sincere manner. The following are ways to help begin this process of reaching out to your son or daughter, or to other teenagers with whom you generally come in contact.

Positive Ways to Help

☐ Treat teenagers who seem depressed in a normal manner.

☐ Encourage them to share their thoughts and feelings.

☐ Show that you care and value them.

☐ Share similar unpleasant experiences that ended positively to provide a basis for hope.

☐ Offer praise and compliments.

☐ Do not criticize or blame depressed teenagers for their bad feelings.

☐ Acknowledge the pain and suffering. It is easy to get impatient and angry with someone who is depressed. This is not a time to prove to them that you are right. Make it clear that you are genuinely concerned about their feelings.

☐ The possibility of suicide is always there. Talks, threats, and attempts at hurting oneself need to be taken seriously.

TALKING TO DEPRESSED TEENS

Talking to teenagers who are depressed can be exasperating and frustrating. This is especially true when they are struggling and upset. It is often easier to become critical or moralistic about their behavior than to acknowledge their suffering. It is also easier to avoid their poor attitudes and to focus on others who are more enjoyable to be around. With a helping hand and encouraging words, depressed teenagers can be helped.

What to Do

- **IF** you think your teenager or teenagers you know have very low self-esteem or tend to be self-critical

  TRY giving them frequent and genuine praise, accentuate their positive characteristics, supportively challenge their self-criticism, and point out their negative thinking patterns.

- **IF** your family situation changes

  TRY to maintain routine and to discuss any changes beforehand in order to reduce worry.

- **IF** you see your teenager or teenagers you know begin to act unusually helpless or show signs of feeling hopeless

  TRY having them write down or express their immediate feelings and focus on any of their pleasant thoughts throughout their day and week.

- **IF** you notice that your teenager is beginning to have appetite and weight problems

  TRY preparing his or her favorite foods and making mealtime a pleasant occasion.

  DON'T try to force your teenager to eat.

- **IF** your teenager is having trouble sleeping

  TRY engaging him or her in relaxation activities, such as reading or listening to soft music, before bedtime.

  DO help your teenager keep regular bedtime hours.

  DO end the day on a "positive note."

- **IF** your teenager is showing signs of agitation and restlessness

TRY changing their activities that might be causing agitation and encouraging physical exercise and recreational activities.

- **IF** your teenager is becoming excessively fearful

  TRY to minimize those situations that may be causing them undo anxiety and uncertainty and be supportive of their expressed concerns.

- **IF** your teenager becomes overly aggressive and extremely angry

  TRY to convey a kind but firm message that the expression of angry feelings is acceptable but destructive behavior is not.

  DO not react to anger with anger.

- **IF** your teenager is having problems in concentration and thinking

  TRY to encourage increased participation in games, activities, and discussions around the house and to work with the teachers and school counselor to promote learning.

BEING A CONCERNED PARENT

As concerned parents, it is extremely important for you to listen and watch for the signals that your teenagers give off to let people know that they are feeling upset or depressed. These are the same behaviors, though, that usually offend others and increase their problems. Without assistance, teenagers are bound to fail. Parents need help, too.

With the aid of other parents, teachers, and mental health professionals, the seriousness of your teenager's underlying depression can be accurately evaluated and plans made to improve his or her emotional and behavioral adjustment. It is then that something can be done to overcome the downward spiral that has befallen your teen. It is up to you to begin this process. Although it can be emotionally painful and draining, it is certainly worth the price.

THINGS TO REMEMBER

- Though adolescence is a time of normal ups and downs, most teens traverse this period of life with few severe psychological problems.

Those teens who experience dramatic ups and downs may be suffering from clinical depression.

- Other emotional disorders, such as anorexia or bulimia, anxiety, substance abuse, and disturbances in conduct, can co-occur with teenage depression.

- Adolescents are masters of disguise—it may be difficult for parents to identify the emotional state of their own children.

- Most parents do not want to think of their teenagers as depressed. What they usually see is someone being lazy, out of control, or obnoxious.

- It is important for parents to secure a comprehensive evaluation for their child when symptoms are noticeable. This may begin with a complete physical and then a psychoeducational assessment. With a clear picture of a teen's strengths, weaknesses, and emotional makeup, parents can begin to access the necessary help that their teen needs.

- It often takes a team effort to help a child through the courses of emotional problems during adolescence. Parents should talk openly to friends, teachers, coaches, and clergy. Local mental health organizations can also help families traverse many difficulties. There is much support available for parents and their teen. All you need to do is ask for it.

CHAPTER 7

Teenage Suicide: A Not-So-Secret Killer

NEW YORK, N.Y.—A sixteen-year-old high school student took his life yesterday by overdosing on his father's prescription pills. A quarterback for the varsity football team and a debate team member, he had been on the National Honor Roll for the last two years. . .

THE TRAGEDY OF SUICIDE

Newspapers, magazines, nightly news—accounts of teenage suicide have become almost commonplace. A high school senior with a promising future and a potentially easy acceptance into a coveted Ivy League school is found dead by his own hand. A 15-year-old girl, quiet but well respected by her teachers and peers, is found lying unconscious after an overdose of her parents' medications. Vivid images of youths taking their own lives continue to shock and sadden the public.

Even popular movies like *Ordinary People*, which focused on a depressed and suicidal teenager, and *Dead Poet's Society*, which addressed family miscommunication and the teenager's need for individuation, appear to reverberate this country's concern about the troubled times of today's adolescents. Everywhere, advertisements from private psychiatric hospitals warn that teenagers, "the hidden time bombs," will surely explode if prompt treatment is not sought.

Suicide is one of the leading causes of death among today's adolescents.

A recent newspaper article provided results of a national survey of 11,000 teenagers indicating that 25 percent of the males and 42 percent of the females admitted to having seriously considered suicide. Hardly a household has not been touched in some way by this alarming tragedy.

Why is it that teenagers, on the brink of exciting possibilities and adventures, are killing themselves? Can parents, caregivers, educators, and other concerned adults identify suicide's warning signs and red flags? Is it possible to intervene effectively to prevent teen suicide? Is it possible to establish the groundwork and trust to successfully intervene in a teenager's suicidal thoughts?

The process from identification to intervention to prevention of suicide is difficult, but not impossible. As a parent, you have already made the first crucial step—beginning to familiarize yourself through educational materials on the realities and myths of depression and how, left unchecked, depression can lead to suicide. You may also have entered the dialogue of suicide prevention after hearing about "copycat" suicides or about your child's friend next door who took her life.

DEFINING THE PROBLEM

Suicide and suicidal behavior are generally viewed along a continuum from attempts at self-harm to "actually" killing oneself. Most definitions of *suicide* emphasize intention, although even these definitions cause controversy among social scientists. There are always questionable teenage deaths—some suicidal teenagers may actually place themselves in highly dangerous, precarious situations in which they become victims of accidents or homicides. An example of this phenomenon is a teenager who becomes involved with a known drug dealer and is killed during drug-related activities. Another example may be a teenager who has little self-value or who is preoccupied with sadness and mixes drinking with driving, thus, greatly increasing the chance of involvement in a fatal automobile accident. Some police officers use the term *autocide* to describe fatal car accidents that may have been self-imposed. Due to this gray area in definition, any significant statistic about teenage suicide is an educated guess at best.

Often, people just do not know another's motives for his or her actions. What is known from mental health professionals is that, when teenagers feel suicidal or have suicidal thoughts, they often engage in impulsive behaviors with little concern for their own lives. However, if it is assumed that all accidents or homicidal acts or incidences of drug usage are forms of suicidal behaviors, the result would overrepresent teenagers who are actually suicidal. The reality falls somewhere in the middle of these two extremes. Despite problems in grouping statistical behavior, there are some alarming facts that do speak of suicide as a crisis of large proportions.

FACTS AND FIGURES

Among teenagers in this country, suicide has become one of the top three causes of death, along with accidents and homicides. The rate has tripled in the last 30 years, and there has been a comparable increase in the number of teenagers who attempt suicide and have suicidal thoughts. For teens aged 15 and up, and including college students, it has become the second leading cause of death. Annually since 1977, over 5,000 youths, aged 15 to 24, have killed themselves—about 20 percent of the total number of deaths by suicide. While suicide attempts in the general population outnumber suicide completions by a ratio of 8 to 1, the ratio for youth is 25 to 50 suicide attempts for every 1 suicide completion.

In addition to suicide attempts and suicide completions, there is a third area of consideration—the *suicide crisis*. This refers to those moments or situations when individuals struggle with the idea of suicide, become obsessed with it, and even plan a suicide in detail. Yet many adolescents who experience a suicide crisis come to grips with the intense pain and agony and stop short of an actual attempt. While figures on the number of suicide crises are difficult to discern, it is believed that each year, approximately one million or more young people in this country experience suicide crises of varying degrees.

One study attempted to describe varying characteristics of children and adolescents who had committed suicide. The report identified the following risk factors:

1. Males were overrepresented—by a 4 to 1 margin.

2. Females in the study were more likely than males to have made previous attempts.

3. Older adolescents had the greater likelihood of completing suicide attempts as compared to younger adolescents.

4. The vast majority (94 percent) of the suicide population was white. About 50 percent of the cases studied were also diagnosed as having an emotional disturbance, including depression, substance abuse, conduct disorders, schizophrenia, and bipolar illness.

A large heterogeneity exists when studying individuals who have committed suicide. Almost every teenager seems vulnerable. It may not only be the depressed or emotionally disturbed youth, but also the angry, impulsive, and rule-breaking teenager who is at increased risk for self-destruction.

It is important to emphasize that many teenagers are engaged in rebellious behaviors that may involve high risk activity. This does not mean, though, that every teenager is suicidal. While there may be controversy about measuring suicidal actions, teenagers who are considered at risk for suicide are different from other adolescents because teens who are not depressed spend less time considering violent or self-destructive behaviors.

This does not count those adolescents who go screaming into their room shouting "I would rather die than miss that concert" when a limit has been set on them. These common and most assuredly recognizable interactions between parents and their teens are often precipitated by an argument and, although uncomfortable, do not in and of themselves contribute to suicidal behaviors. Of course, the overriding question still remains—when do we take these statements seriously?

WHY DO PEOPLE COMMIT SUICIDE?

Factors in Suicide

There are countless reasons why people commit suicide. Among those commonly cited are: (a) to find relief from feelings of hopelessness, (b) to escape from a seemingly intolerable situation, (c) to punish loved ones, (d) to gain attention, (e) to change other people's behavior or change one's circumstances, (f) to join a deceased loved one, (g) to avoid punishment, (h) to avoid becoming a burden, (i) to escape the effects of a dreaded disease, (j) to express love, and (k) to pursue an irrational, impulsive whim.

For teenagers, traumatic events, be they real (such as losing a parent), or perceived (such as the breaking off of a relationship, not getting into the college of their dreams, or losing an important competition), may precipitate a suicidal crisis. Such an event may activate longstanding feelings of inadequacy, inferiority, or injustice. Teenagers may begin to feel doomed— that there is no way out of their dilemma, that things could not possibly get better, or that they can no longer bear the thought of continued emotional pain.

Suicide Notes

Notes left by people who have killed themselves usually tell of irresolvable life crises. Many eloquently describe what it is like to endure chronic pain, to lose loved ones, or to lack the money to pay bills or the ability to perform the simplest tasks. The question remains, why does one choose to give up life when most persons in similar circumstance have managed to cling to life through the worst of times?

Study of Suicide

Mental health investigators from varied disciplines have been trying to answer that very question for decades. In recent years, an entire new field of study—suicidology—has grown out of that effort. This emerging field of study explores how disease and genetic factors interact with social, psychological, and environmental factors.

Psychologists have observed that some people conduct their lives in a way that predisposes them to failure and self-destruction. Sociologists point to the social and economic dislocations and resulting alienation that drive some people to suicide. Increasingly, biological investigators are studying how irregularities in brain chemistry affect impulsive and aggressive behavior that often coincides with suicide attempts. All these scientists emphasize that suicide is the result of an everchanging interplay of many different factors.

Triggering Events

When researchers attempt to pinpoint the key stressful, or triggering event surrounding a suicide attempt, they often find such factors as (a) intense family altercations, (b) deteriorating school performance, (c) sudden disappointments, (d) involvement with the legal system, (e) experienced or threatened loss, (f) breaking off of a relationship, and (g) work-related problems. However, it is not these factors individually that increase the risk of suicidal behaviors. Increased risk of suicide occurs when these stressors are combined with an inability to effectively resolve the greater enhancement in tension.

TEENAGERS AT HIGH RISK FOR SUICIDE

When are teenagers in such severe distress that they would want to kill themselves? Why are some more prone than others to using suicide as an option to reduce their pain and suffering? How are their expressed symptoms or behaviors during these times different from ordinary teenage moodiness? These questions can be difficult to answer confidently, but awareness is important for targeting the teens who need extra assistance.

Those Who Have Made Prior Suicide Attempts

Teenagers who have made serious prior suicide attempts are at highest risk for actually killing themselves. The suicide rate for repeat attempters is dramatically higher than the overall rate in the general population. Between 20 percent and 50 percent of the people who commit suicide had previously made attempts.

Drug and Alcohol Abuse

Drug and alcohol abuse and adolescent suicide are tightly allied. It is common to hear about teenagers who have used drugs and/or alcohol before suicide attempts. Drug and alcohol usage can lessen inhibitions toward dangerous activities that may lead to suicidal gestures. It may also intensify aggressive postures and leave teenagers vulnerable to greater feelings of anger. When this anger begins to turn inward, it can lead to increased urges to end the pain through suicide.

Gay and Lesbian Youth

Adolescents struggling with issues of sexuality, homosexuality in particular, are at a higher risk for suicide than their heterosexual counterparts. They are particularly vunerable in late adolescence when issues of sexuality come to a peak. This may make them more prone to depressed thoughts and feelings. Recent research suggests that gay and lesbian youth attempt suicide at a rate two to three times higher than their heterosexual peers.

Cluster or Copycat Suicides

In one affluent suburb, two teens were found dead in their parents' garage, self-poisoned by carbon monoxide. A week later, it was reported that three other teens had independently attempted the same suicide act. Studies have shown that when there is one publicized adolescent suicide, others do tend to follow. Usually, an already vulnerable teen will be triggered by the suicide of another teen into attempting his or her own suicide. One reason for this motivation may be that adolescents are particularly prone to imitate and are easily influenced by peers. This does not mean, however, that responsible discussion of the realities of depression and suicide should be avoided.

Clinical Depression

While 85 percent of depressed people are not suicidal, most suicide-prone individuals are depressed. Thus, paramount in preventing suicide is identifying and treating depression. A person who is depressed, uncommunicative, and withdrawn may be flashing a danger signal. When suicide clues and depression appear against a backdrop of stressful events in a teenager's life, such as the loss of a parent, friend, a serious illness, or a major move, there is even greater concern.

Isolated teens who have poor social ties, abuse alcohol or other drugs, or have a history of physical and emotional difficulties are at even higher suicide risk when in the throes of depression. In those situations, their thinking is often convoluted. Every issue is polarized—yes or no, black or white, life or death. Researchers have pointed to a deficit in the thinking of severely depressed people that is similar to some neurological conditions known to cause thought and memory problems. *Just when people need most to be clear-headed, they are not.*

THE PRECIPITANT FOR SUICIDE

The actual suicide attempt is usually precipitated by an event or incident that is construed as humiliating and excruciatingly painful for the teenager. The most common events include a breakup of a romantic relationship, an arrest, a rejection, or a quarrel with a parent or romantic partner. Sexual abuse and exploitation are also possible precipitants for suicide attempts.

One mother participated in a parental support group while her son was hospitalized for a suicide attempt. "I never knew how painful breakups could be for teens. When Gordon told me his girlfriend had dumped him, I was supportive but told him he'd feel better in the morning. I've learned not to minimize adolescent relationships by viewing them as only puppy love. I realize now how intensely Gordon feels pain."

MYTHS AND FACTS ABOUT TEENAGE SUICIDE

There are many myths that have developed about suicide and the risk of suicide. As a result, many people still do not consider suicide a major problem among the young. In reality, it is a leading cause of death in teenagers. It is vitally important to clarify some of the myths and to educate oneself and others about the truths of suicide.

Myth: Suicidal people are crazy.
Fact: Although a majority of suicidal individuals are depressed, they rarely would be considered insane. Oftentimes, clues to the depression can be subtle, and the teenager will appear quite "normal."

Myth: Teenagers who are seriously considering suicide do not talk about their suicidal thoughts.
Fact: The majority of teenagers speak or give clues about their suicidal contemplations prior to an attempt.

Myth: Teenagers who threaten to commit suicide are unlikely to follow through.

Fact: Though many teenagers who talk about suicide may not actually commit suicide, most teenagers who commit suicide have spoken about their feelings and intentions.

Myth: Teenagers are impulsive and do not actually plan ahead to hurt themselves.

Fact: Many suicides are planned actions that have often been thought through well in advance.

Myth: Teenagers will not try to hurt themselves more than once.

Fact: The majority of people who are successful at committing suicide have made prior attempts.

Myth: Talking about suicide only makes teenagers think about it more often.

Fact: Discussing the topic with teenagers shows them that you care and that you also take them seriously. Public forums on the subject are healthy ways to keep informed and to exchange concerns.

Myth: Teenagers who have attempted suicide really want to die.

Fact: Most teenagers have really not made up their mind. Frequently, they have given signals about how they are feeling in the hope that someone will help them. Often they want to escape current turmoil or pain and cannot think of other solutions.

Myth: Suicidal people rarely have gone for help.

Fact: Many teens have sought or received some help during the months before their deaths.

Myth: The moment a teenager decides to commit suicide, nothing can be done.

Fact: Just the opposite is true. Most people can be stopped, but all attempts to intervene may not be successful. Making the effort is worthwhile.

THINGS TO REMEMBER

- Suicide is a leading cause of death among the nation's teens and *the* major public health concern of teenage depression.
- Older adolescents are more likely to complete a suicide than their younger counterparts.

- Females are more likely than males to attempt suicide, but males are more likely than females to complete a suicide.
- Gay and lesbian youth tend to be more at risk for suicide attempts than their heterosexual counterparts.
- Teenagers do copy what other teens are doing, even when it includes harming themselves.
- Most teenagers send out messages that they are thinking about suicide.
- There are many myths about suicide. The *facts* should be learned.

CHAPTER 8

Suicide: Intervention and Prevention

THE SIGNALS OF TEENAGE SUICIDE

Fevers can easily be measured by a thermometer, but the risk for suicide cannot be as easily assessed. No foolproof instrument exists to indicate who is highly suicidal and who is not. There is no profile or checklist that definitively characterizes a suicidal person. Suicide, like most human behavior, is hard to predict.

However, most suicidal individuals do convey their intentions to someone in their social network, be it friends, family, or co-workers. Sometimes, these messages are overt. Michael, for example, let his supervisor on his paper route know that he had been thinking of killing himself: When asked why he had neglected to deliver the paper the previous three mornings, Michael told Mary, "I can't do it anymore. I need an escape . . . I think being dead is the only answer. You might as well find another paper boy."

In many cases, the clues are more subtle and disguised. Experts cannot say with precision whether a person will or will not commit suicide. Yet, there are several danger signals, particularly when seen in combination, that demand immediate concern and attention.

Parents of potentially suicidal teens must stay informed and must remain watchful observers. The best defense against suicide is awareness and knowledge. Many of the signs of suicide risk overlap with signs of depression for the simple fact that most youths who attempt suicide are indeed

87

depressed. Parents should reach out to a professional trained in recognizing suicide warnings if they have any concerns.

Suicide attempts usually do not happen without some signals that indicate something is wrong. Research states that four out of five people who kill themselves provide many signals of their intentions. It is essential to be alert to these early clues. Parents should take a teenager's suicide attempts and fatalistic statements seriously and should not be afraid to talk openly about their concerns. Even after it seems as if the worst is over, it could be that a teenager may have made the decision to commit suicide. Parents should learn the warning signs and keep them fresh in their minds. The following is a consolidated checklist of the warning signs mentioned in Chapter 7.

Parents' Checklist of Suicide Warning Signs

- ☐ Marked changes in personality.
- ☐ Sudden change in sleeping or eating patterns.
- ☐ Unexplained, significant drop in school or other work responsibilities.
- ☐ Verbal threats of suicide.
- ☐ Loss of interest in usual activities.
- ☐ Social withdrawal.
- ☐ Lack of concern about appearance.
- ☐ Lapses of attention and concentration.
- ☐ Dangerous or illegal activities (running away, drug or alcohol abuse).
- ☐ Recent rejection (from friends, clubs).
- ☐ Giving away or throwing away prized possessions.
- ☐ Explosive outbursts.
- ☐ Reading stories or drawing pictures about death.
- ☐ Possession of dangerous weapons.
- ☐ Unexplained cheerfulness after prolonged depression.

If your teen is showing several of these signs, it is possible that serious problems are occurring. Attempts at suicide may appear foolish, but they can be deadly. Accidents do happen. Don't shy away from teenagers just because you think they are trying to get attention. They *are* trying to get attention and they truly need it. The basic rule in suicide prevention is to DO SOMETHING. It is much better to be wrong in taking action than to not do anything.

WHAT CAN PARENTS DO?

Your most vital role and function as parents of at-risk adolescents is to listen supportively. If a teenager appears depressed and exhibits any of the warning signals, take time to listen and show your caring and concern. When you think that a teenager, especially your own, may be suicidal, it is normal to feel anxious and unsure of what to say. You do not have to feel intrusive by simply stating something like, "You don't seem to be like your usual self." By being direct and showing some concern, you can ask many questions and may receive straight answers.

A troubled youth needs someone who will listen. It certainly is not easy to discuss suicidal thoughts, but it is critical for teens to talk about why they want to die. Every effort should be made to understand the problems behind the statements, even if their reasoning makes little sense. Although you should show interest, refrain from making moral judgments or trying to talk a youth out of it. The value of listening cannot be overrated.

The following checklist of what to do and what not to do reviews and emphasizes the previous points and makes it easier for you to talk to a troubled adolescent:

What to Do

• Trust your own judgment. You must use your own intuition in deciding whether a troubled youth may be self-destructive.

• Offer help immediately, and there will be no need to feel regret later.

• Demonstrate your support. Show that you are concerned and that you do not want him or her to do anything that would be harmful.

• Be open and direct. Be free with your questions. Ask whether active plans have been made. Teenagers who can state how, when, and where they will commit suicide are very serious about carrying out their ideas.

· Remove all potentially dangerous items, such as weapons, pills, or alcohol, from the home. Many teenagers can be impulsive, without realizing the consequences.

· Sometimes you will need extra assistance. Seek help. People such as teachers, school counselors, and clergy are easy to contact and can help resolve problems. You may have to insist on the help or to contact the appropriate people yourself.

What *Not* to Do

· Do not be sworn to secrecy. Suicidal teenagers need help. Losing friendship or trust temporarily is better than losing a life forever.

· Never leave a suicidal person alone. If the risk appears great, stay with the person.

· Do not appear shocked or alarmed by what your teen tells you. You are trying to build a space of confidence and security.

· Do not try to be a therapist. Just listen to your teens' concerns without being judgmental.

· Do not get into a debate over the morals of suicide. You may run the risk of increasing the person's sense of guilt and feelings of sadness.

· Do not point out that other people have worse troubles and that your teen should compare themselves to less fortunate. This can make your teen feel even less competent and understood.

As an active listener, if you feel that your child is in any risk of suicide, contact a mental health professional. Once you have made the contact, the specialist will assess the risk of suicide. It is helpful for parents to be cognizant of the questions and tactics clinicians use to determine risk. Once risk is determined, the clinicians and parents can then make the first steps towards intervention.

DETERMINING THE RISK

Approaching the suicidal teenager is difficult and can take much time and effort. The degree of risk must somehow be determined. Definitive steps must be taken to safeguard the teenager from immediate danger and to monitor his or her behavior. Finally, finding appropriate follow-up counseling is important.

Assessing the Danger

There are a number of specific questions to ask suicidal teenagers to determine their specific intentions. The answers you receive from the following questions will give you a strong indication of the seriousness of the threat.

• "What has been occurring in your life that is making you think of suicide?" or "What happened that has made things so bad for you?"
• "Do you have a plan to end your life?" (Remember, the more specific the plan is about method, place, time, and who will or will not be nearby, the greater the potential for suicide.)
• "On a scale from 1 to 10, how much do you want to live (or die)?"
• "How often do you think about dying?" "Is the feeling strong?" "How long does it last?"
• "Have you or anyone else that you know attempted (or completed) suicide?"
• "Do you know anyone who will try to stop you from committing suicide?"

This last question is important in determining backup support. It is crucial to obtain an answer. Ask for names, addresses, and phone numbers to plan immediate and future precautions. If the risk is determined to be high, then steps toward intervention must be made.

Steps Toward Intervention

The primary goal of intervening with a suicidal youth is to resolve the immediate problems and to mobilize the available resources, whether it be family, friends, or school personnel. In performing these actions, you are giving the message that alternative solutions can be found and that the teenager has more control than he or she realizes. For a positive resolution to occur, a well-coordinated, short-term plan must be established.

For the first 24 to 72 hours, an acutely suicidal teen needs supportive help and direction. An around-the-clock watch is necessary and should be arranged by family and friends staying with the teenager until the immediate crisis subsides. A written agreement with suicidal teenagers stating that they will not harm themselves during this time is often helpful. This contract should be specific in identifying all the activities and the people who will be around during this time. It should also mention that the person developing the contract will be notified immediately if actions even hinting of suicide persist.

By providing this guidance with confidence and reassurance, a strong message is being delivered that the crisis is short-lived and that a favorable outcome is expected. A foundation has also been laid showing that any future problem can be handled.

THINGS TO REMEMBER

- Though you may feel awkward asking teenagers about whether they are thinking about suicide, it is far safer to ask and to make your concerns clear than to risk an attempt.
- Suicidal teens usually do raise "red flags" that indicate what they have in mind. It is important that you are aware of these signs and symptoms.
- If you have any thoughts that your teen is suicidal, remove any firearms from the house (do not just "hide" them in the house) and keep all medication locked in a secure place.
- Contact a mental health professional if you have any concerns that your child is suicidal.

CHAPTER 9

The Family's Influence on Depression and Suicide

Mary

Mary, aged 16, was failing school, became truant, and often lied to her parents about her whereabouts. She also began to experiment with a variety of drugs. Following an argument with her mother, Mary threatened suicide. The mother, who was feeling overwhelmed and beginning to withdraw from her investment in the family, became distraught at this threat. The father, who was trying to hold the family together, initiated a call to a counseling center.

With the mother becoming more fragile, she announced after an outburst by Mary that she would no longer attend counseling sessions. During the following sessions, it was learned that the mother had a serious drinking problem and had been emotionally absent from the family for the better part of the previous two years. It was feared by Mary, but denied by the father, that the mother was involved with another man. Whenever Mary began getting into trouble, the father attempted to intervene, but her own anger toward the mother would not let him be effective. Mary concurred during the sessions that she was desperate for her mother to "return" to the family and that perhaps her misbehavior was a way to get through to her mother. The threat of suicide seemed to her the only solution because of her feelings of abandonment and lack of other meaningful alternatives.

Through the counseling sessions, Mary began to gain an appreciation for her father's plight and to see that he was doing his best to help her. Through their work together, they were able to coordinate their efforts in order to get the mother off her alcohol dependency and reinvested in the family.

Barbara

Barbara, a 15-year-old girl, was placed in a psychiatric unit of a general hospital after having run away with her boyfriend and then overdosing on her mother's antidepressant medication upon returning home. Barbara lived with her mother, a younger brother (aged 11), and a younger sister (aged 6). Her parents had divorced four years previously, and her father had moved out of town.

During the past several years, Barbara had taken on considerable responsibility not only in raising her younger siblings, but also in providing emotional sustenance to her mother.

This role reversal affected her school performance and her ability to maintain close peer contact. Her isolation within the home also brought her relationship with her mother overly close and dependent, with no room to explore on her own.

When a court arrangement gave her father custody of her brother, Barbara became exceedingly angry at her mother for what she perceived as a betrayal of trust. In seeing her mother still too weak to fight and acknowledging her own feelings of helplessness, she chose to escape the dilemma by running away. Upon Barbara's return home, her mother attempted to elicit guilt over what she saw as another person leaving her. Caught in this bind, Barbara went to the medicine cabinet and took an overdose of pills.

INTERPERSONAL FACTORS OF DEPRESSION AND SUICIDE

In Chapter 5, some of the individual reasons for depression were explored from both psychological and biological perspectives. Yet some social scientists emphasize that the causes of depression and suicide are as much or even more related to interpersonal reactions than to individual characteristics.

Adolescents do not live in a vacuum. They are integrally a part of their family. They rely on their family for nurturance, shelter, care, values, and a sense of belonging. Family influences also can work to create and sustain depression in adolescents.

This chapter takes a look at the meaning of "normal" family functioning and then explores some ways that family dynamics contribute to adolescent depression and suicide. Like the previous discussions of depression, this chapter does not imply that the family is the sole cause of depression; the family is only one of many influences that may affect the depressed adolescent, but it is a very important one in maintaining the symptoms and possible suicidal crises.

ARE THERE REALLY "NORMAL" FAMILIES?

Before examining the family influences that may cause or sustain depression in a teen, it is helpful to examine the so-called "normal" functioning of a family in the grips of raising an adolescent. Adolescents are straddling childhood and adulthood. It is natural for this significant time of transition to impact the family and to cause waves in an otherwise fairly calm domestic sea.

Parents, too, have many changing roles: (a) not being the authority figures and main influences, (b) relinquishing their influence as children become adolescents, (c) recognizing their adolescents' independence, and (d) having a less active role in their child's development. For both parent and adolescent it is a time of change. There is a necessary struggle in renegotiating family roles and expectations.

A normal family establishes a balance between independence and dependence. Parents of adolescents recognize that their child's coming-of-age issues may trigger some of their own unconscious adolescent issues. And the family must also work at pursuing new role definitions. The families that recognize these issues and talk about them are deemed "healthy."

An Example

Joan Normal called up her neighbor one afternoon. "Karen is driving me crazy!" she said. "Last week she asked me if I would go shopping with her to choose a dress for the prom. Today, I was getting ready to take her shopping and she said offhandedly, 'Oh, Mom, did I tell you that Alice (her classmate) is going to help me pick out my dress?' Sometimes I feel needed, the next moment I feel redundant!"

Joan feels frustrated by this push and pull of Karen's maturity, but she can recognize it as part of the process of growing independence. Joan reaches out to her friends for the support, venting, and perspective she needs. Joan also has recognized, painfully, that when she was an adolescent, she was not socially sought after; very few boys were interested in her romantically. Watching Karen's experience, she feels happy that Karen has lots of friends and potential boyfriends. But, she also feels oddly jealous of her daughter's ease and comfort in social situations. She and also her husband find time to talk about their reactions concerning their soon-to-be-adult child.

Even though all families must weather a certain degree of perplexity during this time, some families are more vulnerable to change, and struggle more profoundly in negotiating this change These families may foster an environment that creates or maintains depression.

FAMILIES VULNERABLE TO DEPRESSION

Genetic Predisposition and Family History

Evidence suggests that one's genetic makeup and family history have a strong impact on whether an adolescent might exhibit suicidal behavior; that is, if a family member suffers from depression or one has committed suicide, then an adolescent in the family is more likely to commit suicide. This greater risk factor is probably due both to the identification with the suicidal family member and to the general genetic transmission of psychiatric disorders. So, if Uncle Harry attempted suicide, this could increase the chances that an adolescent in the family might attempt suicide because of: (a) a possible genetic link for depression or (b) the identifying with this uncle and the modeling of the behavior.

Having relatives from either present or past generations that have taken their own lives presents a powerful message to the surviving members—that suicide is at least one viable option of overcoming undue stress. One recent investigation found that almost half of the 243 suicidal patients studied had a family history of suicide.

Unresolved Losses

Issues surrounding unresolved losses have also been found to be key ingredients in determining which families and youngsters are at risk of depression and suicide. A teenager's extreme reactions can result from disruptions that have previously occurred or are presently happening to the family. The teenager may not be reacting to an actual loss, such as the death of a parent, but to an emotional experience of loss. These sensations may be experienced over parental divorce or separation, or over withdrawn involvement or affection that was once previously expressed. When these feelings are kept inside, inappropriate attempts at exposing this felt pain are likely to appear during times of later stress.

These feelings of incompleteness can even be filtered down through generations, with the repercussion of the teenager "acting out" the unresolved grief for a parent.

An Example

Judy, a young teenager, was brought into treatment because of statements that she would be "better off dead" so that others would no longer be bothered by her actions.

In discussions with her parents, it was discovered that Judy's maternal grandmother had committed suicide and that Judy's mother had always felt somehow responsible for the death. Because of this tragedy, the mother feared getting close to anyone, even her daughter. The mother's greatest fear was that she would ruin other people's lives—just like she ruined her mother's.

With her emergence of adolescence, Judy began to feel guilty for appearing to be a burden to her mother; but, at the same time she felt angry about her mother's reluctance to get involved with her. Additionally, it was during this time that both parents began to fight about their differences over how much freedom to give Judy. Judy was caught in the escalation of her parents' discord, and she began to feel hopelessly unable to move on with her own life outside of the home; she felt ineffective and worthless.

Without being able to resolve prior losses, general issues of adolescence concerning attachment and nurturance often get played out at heightened levels. Suicidal actions can become the ultimate demonstration of that rejection. Loss that was once experienced can reappear when the original source of the conflict is not resolved.

Significant Losses

A crucial factor of heightened risk in teenage suicides is the exposure to a parental death before the age of 12. Although other emotional losses, such as parental separation or divorce, can plague a teenager, it appears that a parental death plays a significant role as a predictor in those teenagers who have attempted suicide. Severe family disruption can cause a vacuum in an emerging identity and leave a sense of isolation within teenagers. This hole in their background contributes to the outlook that they truly have no control over their environment.

The loss of a parent early in life has removed or displaced a crucial role model at a critical time in development. This seems to have a profound impact upon teenagers' self-esteem, making them more suggestible to peer influence and hindering their skills in obtaining mature relationships. It also has the effect of precipitating increases in anxiety and depression.

Besides the physical and emotional loss of a parent, the psychological loss brought on by neglect, discord, abuse, or illness can also have a major impact as a predictor for those at risk for suicide. Studies have shown that within families where a suicide has occurred, there tends to be an increased rate of medical or psychiatric illness; especially present is substance abuse and a family history of suicide.

Factors that allow teenagers to overcome significant losses in their life are dependent on: (a) whether the loss stemmed from death, divorce, or desertion; (b) their age when the loss was experienced; (c) their own internal strength; (d) their ability to have achieved independent functioning; and (e) the amount of available support within the family. One study of suicidal youths found that 75 percent had experienced a significant loss or an anniversary of a loss within several weeks of their attempts.

Miscommunication

Battles over freedoms and limits place families with teenagers at risk. The inability of parents and teenagers to verbally express what it is occurring or how they genuinely feel about the changes in their lives is another marker for depression. A stressful family environment becomes exacerbated when family members fail to communicate clearly and to understand one another, especially during times of difficulties or crises. It is often the case during these times of conflict, that breakdowns of communication occur and that one or more of the family members feel excluded.

John's parents, beginning to feel threatened by his demands, joined together so tightly that they no longer gave John the space in their relationship that was previously accorded. As a result, John felt "boxed out," excluded and abandoned even from his father with whom he had previously enjoyed a close relationship.

The act of suicide is the ultimate expression of both anger and hopelessness. When teenagers sense that their usual channels of communication are blocked and ineffective, they start to feel desperate and begin to panic. As their own inner tension and uncertainty escalates, they may begin to engage in highly destructive behaviors. In these instances, self-injurious behaviors may reflect their turmoil and the distorted perception that their identity is being consumed or lost. When, on the other hand, all family members feel alienated and disengaged from one another, suicidal attempts can be viewed as extreme reactions or "pleadings" to be heard.

Although these factors may increase the likelihood of suicidal actions among family members, they alone do not cause the act of suicide but merely contribute to increased stress. When they are added to other characteristics of the potentially suicidal adolescent, such as extreme anger, sadness, or previous exposure to suicidal behavior, they do paint a foreboding picture.

Boundaries Within Families

Depression and suicidal behaviors are typically seen in families where boundaries between family members, or between the family and the community, are either extremely arbitrary or rigid. A suicide attempt could be merely a teenager's cry for help, protesting the family's rigidness or the family's lack of support and attention to the child at risk for suicide.

One example is Samantha, whose family tended to stay to themselves in their small community. Samantha's father was in the military, and, when the family was posted overseas, the few contacts Samantha had in her community were cut off. She felt she had no outlet and no one to listen to her problems. When her worries began to lead to anger towards the family, she began to feel intensely guilty. As a result, Samantha cried out for help—by slashing her wrists.

The "Parentified" Child

An equally stressful dilemma for teenagers occurs when they are placed in a "parentified" role. This happens when the roles that are usually specific to the child (dependence on the parent for life's needs) are taken by the adult and the child becomes the caretaker and provider of nurturance for the parent and other family members. Since the teenager still has strong dependency needs, this added burden of the caretaker role creates a conflict that may result in a desperate suicide attempt.

In the example at the beginning of the chapter, Barbara's unresolved and unanticipated losses, combined with being in the predicament of a role reversal, caused an untenable position for Barbara. She was caught between competing forces, needing her own independence, yet bound to her home and responsibility for her mother's emotional well-being.

Barbara also never had the opportunity to work through her father's leaving her and taking with him Barbara's brother, who in this role reversal, had become more of a son to her. The events leading up to her depression and suicide attempt were created by the emotional conflict (dissonance) of being deprived of the age appropriate nurturance, and of the few alternatives that she had at her disposal to communicate her distress.

Suicide as a Method of Conflict Resolution

Within families, the inability to articulate difficulties, modulate feelings, and resolve resulting conflicts may lead to despair that culminates in suicidal behaviors. Family members who are prone to suicide attempts are often characterized as intensely disagreeable. The intensity and chronic nature of the unresolved conflicts leave an environment perceived by teenagers as unsupportive, highly stressful with little personal control, and lacking in harmony. Within this strained climate, possibility for change is seen as nonexistent, and the only perceived way out is through emotional withdrawal or an act of finality, like suicide.

Families unable to successfully work through problem areas and to resolve everyday crises create strife and disruption for all family members. It is common to hear from depressed and suicidal teenagers that their families have been beset by conflict for long periods of time.

With the children's emergence as teenagers in this negative atmosphere, the fighting usually escalates due to issues of control. At a time when teenagers are normally attempting to struggle for their own independence, they can tax the fragile family beyond its own limits. Extremes in reactions (i.e., suicide attempts) are often the end result. Although a fight with a family member often precipitates the actions leading to the self-destruction, it is but one more instance of a long chain of disagreements that adds extra tension to the immediate crisis.

CREATING WALLS TO COMMUNICATION

When normal communication channels between parents and their children are blocked, fragmented, or never established, a stressful climate within the household is created. This has the impact of placing family members at risk for "acting out" their grievances. There are countless ways that these faulty patterns in relating can be expressed. Some of these are discussed in the following sections.

Ignoring Each Other

At times, certain signals in communication can encourage depressed feelings and suicidal actions in children and teenagers. Ignoring signs that a teenager in the family may be in severe distress and may even be expressing suicidal thoughts could lead to an already depressed youth attempting suicide. It can make parents highly anxious to hear such negative words being muttered. Yet they may, unwittingly, turn away or interrupt their teenager whenever such a topic is brought up instead of listening to the hurt inside.

It is also not uncommon to actually give verbal cues sanctioning suicide. Often, parents have a difficult time accepting feelings of depression or hopelessness from their child at any age. This blocking of unpleasant feelings can actually increase a teenager's sense of isolation and frustration over not being heard. A suicidal gesture during these times is usually seen as an attempt to break down the walls so that the parents can no longer deny the desperation of their distraught child.

Protecting Each Other

In cases where a parent is physically ill, there is often a nonverbal agreement that neither the parents nor the children will openly express their emotional problems. There is an air of protection that hovers over everyone in the household: "Can't you see that your mother is sick!" For parents with mental illness, children attempt to develop communication skills that help them survive within negative parental interactions. However, these skills in trying to communicate become ineffectual and counterproductive to the children as they grow older.

Expendable Children

Some parents may formulate a conscious or unconscious belief system that a particular child has become bad or an unnecessary burden. When parents communicate feelings of rejection, they have the potential for initiating a "death wish" within the child. When teenagers are faced with such blame and animosity, they often express the parents' wish of "good riddance" through self-destructive or high-risk behaviors. Since the parents are conveying the wish that they would be better off without this child, the teenager is more likely to oblige.

WHEN COMMUNICATION BECOMES A BARRIER

People like to think of communication as a bridge between people. If healthy communication skills are not taught to children at young ages, however, walls are created between children and adults that are exaggerated during the teenage years. The following are examples of faulty communication patterns that can develop within families, thus, interfering with more constructive sharing of ideas and feelings.

Separation Among the Generations

When the belief has been formed that one generation has little to offer another, mistrust can be created. Such often-heard statements as "Life was never that easy when I was your age—you've got everything! What more could you possibly want?" "What do parents know about sex?" "What could he possibly know at such a young age?" are certain impediments to optimum listening skills. In these situations, everyone has an opinion, but no one is hearing the other.

Labeling and Criticizing

Parents will often label a misbehavior *bad* believing that the teenager will magically see what is going on and then change the problematic behavior. When this occurs, parents mistakenly feel they have done their job. In reality, they have distanced themselves from their child and denied any of their own responsibility.

The usual results of criticism are frustrated teenagers with lowered self-esteem, which undercuts their motivation for healthy growth. Such putdowns include calling a teenager "stupid," "a bum," "troublebial," " brat," or "clown." Also, one parent blaming a teen for the other parent not being involved or leaving allows little eagerness for change.

Being continuously ignored or criticized contributes to low self-esteem in a teenager and builds the proverbial wall between generations. The teenager who is continually put down or scolded by their parents will likely start living up to these negative expectations.

Constructing Power Plays

Parents and teenagers many times attempt to control the other through ordering, prescribing, and/or lecturing behaviors.

1. Instances where *ordering* is used include those times when the parent is trying to exert influence (e.g., "Because I said so," "Stop moaning and get out and do something," "Stop the antics, I don't want to see or hear you right now").

2. *Prescribing* takes the form of explanation, for instance, parents telling their teenager that they are lazy or are not working as hard as they could.

3. *Lecturing* may include telling a teenage girl that she would not have been in such a mess if she had listened to you in the first place or telling a

teenage boy who has broken up with a friend that there are "other fish in the sea."

Typical responses from teenagers during these interactions may include closing their parents off by (a) agreeing to do it "in a minute" or (b) just becoming angry. These interactions carry strong messages that teenagers lack control in exerting personal competence and that their feelings are being ignored or are unimportant. The resulting breakdown in communication is a signal that neither side is listening or attempting to understand the other.

Social Status

Some parents are so concerned about their own position in the community that they become preoccupied with worrying over their teenagers' imperfections. When parents perceive that their teenagers are beginning to stray from their rules or standards, they begin to nag, ridicule, or withhold rewards. Of course, this only intensifies the tension and produces few desirable results.

In fact, it often produces opposite reactions; the teenagers no longer listen to their parents, and they go out of their way to embarrass their parents and to rebel. At this point, the teenagers are beginning to feel used and often feel as if they are being treated like objects. Resentment quickly builds, and the teenagers feel they can no longer turn to their parents for emotional support and acceptance.

Parents in this situation may feel that they need total control of their teenagers and are confused and angry that their teenagers do not accept their ideas and values. Teenagers in these instances begin to form the belief that their parents are only concerned about what others are thinking and have little tolerance for their teens' own uniqueness. If these teenagers begin to struggle for their own independence, the parents feel threatened and see their children as ungrateful or rebellious, while, conversely, the teenagers see their parents as rigid and unapproachable.

Common interchanges may include direct statements as "What will the neighbors think?" or "Their daughter got an A in that course; what's the matter with you!" By contrast, teenagers can also use the same tactics by commenting that their parents are not "with it" or they are not as fair as their friend's parents.

Double Messages

Saying one thing and meaning or doing another is always a source of confusion between parents and teenagers. It is especially difficult for teenagers to live in households where messages are not clear. Teenagers are testing out various roles and behaviors; and, without clear-cut expectations to fall back upon, they find these transitional years extremely difficult.

A double message can interfere with accomplishments and can place the teenager in Catch-22 situations. Often parents can unconsciously give double messages because they do not anticipate a reaction or because they underestimate the importance of their words. Such statements as "You can go, but I will worry the entire time," or "It's no big deal that you are second or third team," cloud the issue of what is being said. The teenager who is getting involved in a difficult activity may interpret the message by not putting forth a maximum effort to succeed because he or she wants to reduce the parent's worrying. The teenager may feel unloved or not worthwhile unless he or she has made a significant achievement.

Of course, teenagers give many mixed signals to cloud their own true feelings. This is especially true when they feel depressed or suicidal: They may begin to display many signs of distraction or withdrawal from usual interests and activities, but they strongly deny the underlying sadness when confronted about their mood changes.

It is difficult to communicate with teenagers whose actions or statements are conveying one message and who adamantly deny the feelings behind the actions or statements. It is during these times that adults or peers pull away from a teen because of their own frustration in not getting the teenager to discuss his or her true feelings. The teenager then becomes the most vulnerable for carrying out suicidal plans.

Overreacting and Underreacting

When a parent overreacts to a child's message, it can cause the child such distress that he or she will be less likely to talk with that parent in the future for fear of upsetting them. This blocks the potential for shared problem solving and intimacy between parent and child. It also establishes a pattern for the child to seek solace from peers instead of adults, which can ultimately leave the parent frustrated.

A different kind of overreacting is shown when the parent begins to ask countless questions of the teenager. Although the parent believes the questions express love and concern, the adolescent is likely to perceive them as intrusive and threatening. The teenager becomes turned off. Often, it is better to ask only selected questions and allow the teenager room for openly communicating the concern. Asking questions may only misdirect the conversation from what the teenager really wants to say.

On the other hand, underreacting to a teenager's concern minimizes the importance the teenager has attached to the matter. Parents who tell their teenager not to worry or that something does not matter may convey the idea that they do not want to become involved or just do not understand. Underreacting also is shown through nonverbal gestures such as continuing to read the newspaper or watch television or just not actively listening to the teenager's concerns.

WHAT PARENTS CAN DO—IDENTIFYING POSITIVE COMMUNICATION

When do you know that healthy communication is occurring? First, there is a balance between listening and talking. It is one thing to feel like you are accepting your teenager; it remains quite another for the teenager to feel your acceptance. It is even better if there is a corresponding balance between verbal and nonverbal interchanges. Allowing a teenager to attempt something on his or her own without intervention, as long as it is safe and acceptable, goes a long way toward building self-confidence and acknowledging a child's worth.

Even those times when an adult listens without adding his or her "two cents" can establish a sense that the teenager's ideas and concerns are worthwhile. In the course of the conversation, small continuances or invitations to say more, such as "Tell me more" or "I'd like to hear more," can add much depth to the messages being exchanged and can show deep caring.

Active listening, that is, attempting to understand what the teenager is feeling, elicits more potential for open communication. By parents putting into their own words what they understand the teenager to be saying and feeling *and* by allowing for a response and reaction, any confusion or misunderstandings can be cleared up. An example of this kind of interchange might include the father requesting a chore to be done, the teenager complaining that she always has to do it, then the father acknowledging the anger and providing a reason (e.g., "You are angry because I did not ask anyone else"). The teenager may then identify that she is angry because she feels that she is the only one doing any of the chores.

Ideally, parents should use their everyday conversational tones when talking to their teenagers, but unfortunately this is not always the case. Parents may be tired or stressed and then displace their frustration or anger onto their teenagers. However, parents' tone when providing explanations or asking questions of teenagers should be similar to what it is when talking to other adults. Simply asking open-ended questions, those requiring expanded answers rather than just "yes" or "no," is an excellent beginning to positive and productive communication.

SUMMARY

This chapter has touched on some of the factors that seem to be make some families more vulnerable to depression and suicide than others. Those factors are not absolute, and countless other reasons may play a part in the precipitants toward suicide. The factors that have been detailed, however, do suggest some vulnerabilities that should be considered when dealing with depression and suicidal crises in your own families. As parents, you cannot change your family's genetic makeup or alter your family history; but you can look at your communication within your own families, identifying patterns, strengths, and areas for growth.

THINGS TO REMEMBER

- Family influences, along with psychological and biological causes, can play a role in the maintenance of depression in teens.
- All families have the challenge of negotiating new roles, struggling with issues of independence versus dependence, and understanding the impact of parents' own adolescent issues.
- Families that are particularly vulnerable to changes during adolescence include families with a history of depression, unresolved past

traumas and losses, difficulties in communication and structure, and families that have a difficult time coping with emotions.

- Parents have the power to change how their family is communicating and functioning. This flexibility also offers a model to children on how to cope with difficult times. Parents should be aware of their daily interactions with their children and should address each other's concerns in a thoughtful and caring manner.

PART THREE

Treatment Considerations

CHAPTER 10

Evaluating the Depressed Teenager

Rachel

Rachel was 17 years old when her father brought her to a psychologist for an evaluation. He was perplexed by her sudden drop in grades, her irritability towards him and her younger brothers, and her sudden weight loss. The mother had died several years before, and Rachel had been taking over much of the role as housekeeper in addition to keeping up with her schoolwork. Always a fine and responsible student, she had received acceptance to a prestigious college and was making plans for graduation and leaving home. Lately, however, she seemed preoccupied and conflicted. At weekend parties, she had begun to drink to intoxication. Her excitement toward going to college had been tempered by her anxiety about leaving her family. Also, her father had announced that he had decided to remarry.

After Rachel was seen by a psychologist with her family in an interview, she was interviewed alone and administered scales to assess the degree of her apparent depression and to measure any disturbance in her thinking. Through this process, it was discovered that she had been harboring very distorted views of herself and her situation and had even been considering suicide.

Robin

Robin, aged 15, had been struggling in school for many years. Since she was pleasant and seemed to try, everyone just thought that she was a slow learner.

When she began to complain about physical ailments, her parents allowed her to stay home from school. However, when she began to avoid longstanding friends and ignored party invitations, her parents became more concerned. Upon the recommendation from their family physician, they arranged for her to undergo a psychological evaluation.

The examination discovered that Robin had a significant learning disability that made it difficult for her to read and write. Through the years, this had made Robin become very passive towards her educational pursuits. When she reached high school, she was beginning to feel quite inferior to her peers and no longer wanted to participate with them. Her disability had never before been detected, and it had robbed her of much of her spirit. She had now internalized a very low opinion of herself and was fearful of competing with others, both academically and socially. Her withdrawal was a significant signal to her parents that something was wrong. With the documentation that the psychological testing provided, she was able to gain the necessary assistance in her school to overcome many of her deficits.

PSYCHOLOGICAL EVALUATION

The previous chapters have emphasized possible causes and the debilitating effects of teenage depression. However, since depression is often overlooked as a primary cause in the problematic behaviors of troubled youth, an accurate diagnosis becomes essential. Except for the diagnostic criteria of symptoms, ways of accurately testing for depression and its extent on a child's functioning have yet to be explored.

This chapter will focus on the psychological evaluation as a vehicle for supplying this much-needed information. Assessment by a trained psychologist is crucial to the teenager's parents, physician, and school to document the specific problem areas and offer treatment recommendations.

A psychological evaluation presents a description of an individual's current level of intellectual and emotional functioning. This evaluation is carried out through careful observations of problem-solving strategies and interpersonal skills and through the measurement of ability levels on a series of specially constructed tests. Tests of intelligence and personality are used to look at various aspects of cognitive and emotional resources. Questionnaires are completed by both the teenager and the parents to objectively measure levels of activity, any deterioration in adjustment, or the possibility of suicidal thoughts. The end result offers a profile of a person's strengths and weaknesses in all facets of everyday behavior.

A comprehensive psychological evaluation helps detail the problem areas that may be interfering with a teenager's growth and development. This is especially important when looking at factors that might attribute to low self-esteem, a lack of motivation, or other aspects of depression. When completed, treatment directed at these vulnerable areas can then begin.

Many parents, exasperated by their teenager's poor grades or poor social skills, might not want to put undue pressure on their child and, thus, ignore the possibility that a learning disability or a mood disturbance might be hindering better performance. A thorough psychological assessment can tell parents whether their teenager simply cannot do what is expected of him or her or just will not, because he or she does not want to look bad in front of peers. The testing allows parents the necessary information to make a sound decision about treatment or other kinds of specialized assistance that may be needed.

As the opening examples of depressed teenagers illustrate, the need for accurately assessing the degree and nature of adolescent disturbance is varied, but also unique. While Rachel's image of herself and her importance to her family had been skewed due to the untimely death of her mother, Robin's poor self-concept stemmed from the longstanding impact of her learning problems. In both cases, the need for an evaluation was imperative to specifying the degree of disturbance and to making sound decisions about treatment. A psychologist's analysis of the test scores, in addition to skilled clinical judgment, can answer many questions and mysteries. The results can provide a solid basis for decision making.

DEVELOPMENTS IN ASSESSING TEENAGE DEPRESSION

During the past decade, not only has there been a renewed interest in describing child and adolescent mood disorders, but also numerous questionnaires and interview formats have been constructed that focus on pre-adult depression. These have included formalized interviews, child behavior rating scales and checklists, and questionnaires developed specifically to objectively assess teenage depression and suicidal thoughts and feelings. Psychologists involved in assessment and diagnosis also make judgments about the degree of emotional disturbance by using various indicators on more standard tests such as the Rorschach, the Thematic

Apperception Test (TAT), and assorted subscales of personality inventories, such as the Minnesota Multiphasic Personality Inventory (MMPI).

For the parents, it is essential to find a credentialed, licensed psychologist who specializes in the assessment of adolescents. This clinician must be skilled and comfortable in interviewing teenagers and must have a broad understanding of the developmental reasons that may contribute to the problems. This becomes important (as the parents can readily attest) when faced with depressed teenagers who may generate negative and frustrating responses from adults by their sad moods, lack of interest, oppositional stance, and sometimes open hostility.

WHERE TO FIND QUALIFIED EXAMINERS

Training

It takes a well-trained and qualified examiner to test teenagers. Whether a particular teenager is suffering from a depressive disorder can require subtle discriminations among the various results. The evaluator must understand how certain emotional problems or learning difficulties may manifest themselves during these possibly troublesome years.

These abilities and judgments take experience; so, in addition to solid credentials, it is essential that evaluators have a number of years' experience working with adolescents. Training *and* experience really do matter when it comes to testing teenagers! Only an experienced examiner can provide the comfort needed to allow guarded and distrustful teenagers to produce sincere answers in attempting to describe their distress.

What to Ask

Evaluations are expensive and health insurance plans may or may not cover them. Thus, parents should call and ask questions before committing to an evaluation. It is okay to be assertive; most psychological examiners are used to being questioned and are respectful of families' needs.

Having the questions written down before the phone conversation ensures that all the desired information will be obtained. The questions can be specific to the examiner's degree, licensing credentials, experience with testing adolescents, contact with "normal" adolescents, and professional affiliations. Other pertinent questions may include the total time for the evaluations, and certainly, the costs. Phone calls also give parents the opportunity to gain an initial impression of several examiners and to make comparisons among them.

It is also important to ask whether costs include a follow-up visit with the examiner to review the results and implications for treatment. This is a crucial part of the process that is not always included. It is indeed a valuable and useful session to answer lingering questions about your teenager's problems.

Getting Your Teenager to a Psychologist

You are a parent. You have received enough information to allow you to make decisions about seeking an evaluation and about choosing an examiner. You have made plans to have your teenager evaluated, and now it is time to make sure he or she is willing to go. Although your teen may have given lip service toward agreeing with the assessment, expect him or her to provide some resistance before going.

Teenagers are great at putting their parents on the defensive and making them feel guilty. They may try to bow out or cajole you. They are likely to put down the tests (e.g., "Testing is only for dummies") or say that they have already taken the tests at school. It is best to review again the reasons you want the evaluation. It is also a time to be brief and firm, as there is no reason to get into an argument.

THE EVALUATION

The initial part of the evaluation is usually spent with you, the parents, to clarify any concerns and to discover what you expect from the results. You may be asked to complete questionnaires relating to your teen's childhood history, and to share your views of the problems and levels of distress. In some cases, the psychologist will want to spend time with all family members before actually doing the testing. Psychologists may do this to gain a fuller appreciation of the family and their possible influences on the teenager's behaviors.

When it is time for the testing to be completed, parents and siblings will be asked to leave the room. Since the evaluations can take two to three hours, you may want to leave and return, although most parents are too nervous to leave the office and are highly curious about what is taking place.

Knowing what to expect from an evaluation will lessen the anxiety and mystery and will make for more informative results. Although there is bound to be some variation among examiners and their procedures for evaluating a teenager, they take similar forms. Most likely, there will be an interview to establish rapport between the examiner and the teenager. During this time initial observations about the teenager's social skills, interests, and general intellectual level are being made. The examiner can then begin to gain a clearer picture about the teenager's reasoning skills, soundness of judgment, and his or her personal views about the problems concerning why the testing was needed.

Once this process has allowed the teenager to gain some comfort and confidence in the evaluator, the next step is the actual testing. The tests comprise of various checklists, questionnaires, problems to solve, and inventories that attempt to measure the teenager's functioning in comparison to same-age teenagers. Other tests are more unstructured and attempt to gain a picture of the teenager's personality and coping mechanisms. The information derived from all these tests and questionnaires will describe the teenager's developmental stage both in terms of both intellect and emotional maturity.

AFTER THE EVALUATION

What to Do with the Results

Once the testing is finished, the psychologist, if requested, will go over the results with you and your teenager to make sure everyone understands the results of the tests. It is a time to review the reasons for wanting the evaluation and to explore what was discovered through the evaluative process. It is also a time to plan for any needed intervention. Your teenager should be included, for it is he or she that underwent the tests and will be most significantly affected by the recommendations. Even if they made a big fuss about the testing, teenagers are curious as to what others think of them and want to know where they stand in comparison to other teenagers.

One of the first things that the psychologist will want to review is whether there is a discrepancy between what the teenager stated as the problems and what the family viewed as the major source of conflict. In meeting with the family, teenagers often want to clarify their thinking and get the opportunity to be heard. Parents are usually surprised at what they hear. In the case of depressed teenagers, it may be the first time they have openly addressed the issue of suicidal thoughts.

The review meeting is also a time to share the knowledge gained about the teenager's intellectual strengths and weaknesses and to openly talk about problems in learning and the resulting frustrations. Additionally, the psychologist may want to review the teenager's ability to deal with everyday stress and how this may have contributed to his or her recent problems in behavior. Predictions can also be made about what will likely happen if interventions are not actively followed through.

Understanding What You Are Being Told

It is crucial that parents understand what they are being told about their teenager. The psychologist needs to make the results understandable to everyone present at the informing conference. Sometimes, that means you, the parents, have to take an assertive role. Do not hesitate to stop the examiner if his or her words are confusing, too technical, or too general. You and your teenager need to hear it straight. It is awful to leave the conference having thought one thing only to find that your spouse or teenager has thought the opposite. Everything should be clarified, concrete, and applicable.

Some psychologists tend to be too technical in their explanations. Their language is unique to their profession and often must be interpreted to the general public. If such terms as *attention deficit disorder, learning disability, cognitive rigidity,* or *personality style* are mentioned, make sure that everyone defines those terms the same way.

This is not a time to feel embarrassed by displaying ignorance of what is being told to you. It is not up to you to understand the language of a psychologist; it is up to him or her to be understood. Speak up! You have just spent much money for this information, so get your money's worth. Although you may have questions later, make sure you do not leave the session feeling frustrated and thinking that it was a waste of time and money.

Oftentimes, parents leave the evaluation and informing interview thinking they have not learned anything new at all. Usually, you can feel confident about the evaluation if what you hear confirms your suspicions, matches your teenager's school functioning and school achievement scores, and underscores others' opinions of your child. It is generally better and less confusing to hear consistency than a lot of contradictory opinions.

However, the most important questions for you to consider are whether the evaluation and recommendations are truly useful.

- Did the feedback add to your knowledge about your child?
- Did you gain a better appreciation for the seriousness of your child's emotional disturbance or learning disability?
- Are you clear about what steps to take next?
- Are you optimistic at this point that your child and your family can be helped?
- Were the recommendations specific enough to be useful?

If you can answer these questions in a positive manner, then you certainly got your money's worth.

When You Are Still Not Satisfied

You have made the effort to get your teenager evaluated, and listened to the results, and, yet, you still have lingering doubts and questions. What you heard really did not match what you know about your child. After all, you have spent the past 15 or so years with your child. How could the psychologist be expected to know him or her in a few hours? Should you seek another appointment with the same psychologist? Should you get a second opinion? To whom should you turn with the results?

First, call the psychologist again and pursue your doubts. If you can be specific enough over the phone and if you receive further explanations, everything can be settled by this call. You may have felt that the testing did not answer all your questions. You may still need a brief review of the more technical terms or scores. At other times, you may want to have a follow-up conference to pursue options regarding the recommendations.

You have probably been feeling that something has been wrong for a long time, and one conference may not be enough to cover all aspects of your concerns. Also, the recommendations just may not be useful to your specific situation, and you are still feeling puzzled and frustrated.

Gaining Other Opinions

Should another person be consulted? Before going to the expense of seeking another psychologist to reevaluate your child, it may be best to review the results of the testing with the people that already know your child. Have a conference with the school teacher and/or school counselor and share the results of the testing. They are in an excellent position to carry out many of the recommendations, or at least to offer their opinion about the accuracy of the results and the practicality of the recommendations.

Another person to consult would be your child's pediatrician or the family doctor. While this person may not have a direct handle on your child's everyday functioning, he or she can certainly speak to how your child has functioned through the years and to note any deterioration in abilities. This person may also have excellent referral sources because he or she probably interacts with many varied professionals.

After consulting these people, if you or they still have remaining questions about the results and recommendations, it may be time to gain a second opinion. This may be especially crucial if the recommendations mean taking an exceptional step. Perhaps the psychologist strongly believed that your teenager would only be better able to overcome his or her problems in a residential treatment center, and the nearest one is two states away! Then, you may want to get a second opinion from another psychologist.

It is very possible that your teenager may not have to be retested. In fact, retesting would invalidate many of the results because your teenager would be already familiar with the tests. Another psychologist, though, may provide alternative recommendations based on the results or may want to administer different tests to gain additional material. It is also possible that the second psychologist will want to administer different but similar tests to compare the two outcomes. This can only be done if you supply the psychologist with the original testing and explain to him or her why you are seeking this extra input.

THE FINAL OUTCOME

You have done everything possible at this stage for your child. All your questions have been answered satisfactorily; you have gained sufficient knowledge about the test results and have gained a broader awareness of your child's strengths and weaknesses. Now you can proceed to the next step of finding extra assistance or the right placement for your child. The recommendations may have strongly suggested counseling or tutorial assistance. The psychologist may have suggested transferring schools or, in some cases, may have discussed the option of hospitalizing your child if the risk of harm to self or to others was apparent.

Now that you have become familiar with this psychologist, you may want to seek therapy with him or her or to obtain a recommendation for other therapists who are professional colleagues. Specialized schools may be warranted, and, at that point, you may want the assistance of an educational consultant or may want to speak further with the counselor at your child's present school. Whichever direction you choose to follow, you can at least be assured that now you have the knowledge and information to feel empowered about future direction. That is the real reason for a comprehensive psychological evaluation.

THINGS TO REMEMBER

- An accurate diagnosis based on psychological testing can clarify many misunderstandings and provide direction for treatment.
- It is important to find an examiner who has much experience dealing with adolescent issues related to normal developmental changes and school problems.
- There have been many developments in the measurement of depression and the risk for suicide within children and adolescents.
- Psychological testing provides a portrait of your child, showing you potentials, liabilities, and current functioning. It provides documentation needed by schools and other agencies to carry out any recommendations.
- It is important that you understand the results of the testing. Do not leave feeling frustrated. Make sure you spend sufficient time with someone who can explain all the results clearly and concisely. They must make sense to you, or the money you have spent will be wasted.

CHAPTER 11

Bringing Teenagers to Counseling

Matthew

Sixteen-year-old Matthew was referred for counseling by his high school teacher after being chronically absent from school. Matthew had been, until recently, a good student and active in extracurricular activities. During the preceding three months, Matthew had seemed preoccupied, appeared inattentive and distracted in class, and seemed to be withdrawing from his usual friends and activities. Although his teacher did not get the sense that Matthew was using drugs, she knew that something was wrong and called his parents for a conference.

Once there, his parents acknowledged that Matthew had become more distant than usual and had begun talking back and leaving home without saying where he was going. They had not known that he had been missing so many days of school. "We were concerned about him" stated his father, "but I guess we just chalked it up to his being a teenager because he's really never done anything so secretive and flagrant before."

When the teacher mentioned the need to see a counselor, the parents did not take the suggestion seriously. When Matthew continued his secrecy and disrespectful behavior, the parents called for another school meeting to learn more about counseling and to gain some referrals. Their main objective at the meeting was to find out how they were going to be able to get Matthew to a counselor.

John

John, aged 17, was referred for outpatient counseling after spending three weeks in an adolescent unit of a local hospital. His problems that initiated inpatient treatment included school truancy, isolation from peers, and becoming out of control at home. He had also gained a lot of weight over the last several months and appeared somewhat apathetic and uninterested in most teenage activities.

Since he had received considerable therapy in the hospital, he was much more approachable than most teenagers his age. During the first meeting, he listened attentively, yearning to be heard. He related that he had considerable disagreements with his father that sometimes turned to shouting and shoving matches. After these altercations, he would retreat to his room for days at a time, claiming illness. "I get so anxious and aggravated that I just kind of pull into myself, crank up my music, and try to shut out the world." His parents were resigned to his withdrawal, and felt it was not worth the chance of making him angry to force him out of his room.

Although he had experienced great distress over his actions, he seemed incapable of breaking this gridlock and was generally immature in his problem-solving skills. Though bright, he never put forth a great effort at school nor was he interested in his classes. He preferred solitary activities and had few friends or associates. His interests were limited to computer games and his music collection. Reports from the hospital described him as shy and inhibited. He was in great conflict over his need to be dependent on his parents. He generally experienced sad, anxious, and helpless feelings. Recommendations from the hospital included social skill training and family therapy. The family had already begun sessions at the hospital and felt positive that this was the correct way to handle their son's problems.

WHEN YOUR CHILD NEEDS THERAPY

Worrying about your child's physical health is troublesome enough, but your child's emotional well-being can be even more worrisome. While some parents may overreact to their teenager's expressions of sadness, others who are equally concerned believe it should just be ignored and it will pass with time. Often, it becomes a case of simply not knowing what to do.

The question of placing a teenager in therapy has always been somewhat mystifying and clouded with uncertainty. Parents not only have to worry about their teen's problems but also about their concern about being exposed to strangers. Often, by the time they do choose to find a therapist, parents feel like others have been blaming them for being "bad" parents (whether it be their own parents, in-laws, friends, or teachers).

Hopefully, the days of blaming parents for all their children's ills are over. Modern-day thinking acknowledges that, in addition to parenting styles, children's problems can stem from many possible causes: genetic, biological, and environmental differences; varying temperaments; and different learning styles. Often, when the problems are assessed accurately and treated accordingly, they can be resolved in a fairly short time and the related stress is decreased.

PROFESSIONALS WHO WORK WITH TEENAGERS

Therapists who work with children and adolescents are very aware of parents' feelings and concerns. Skilled clinicians try to discuss these feelings and concerns before the actual work is completed. Often, they give you the credit, and justifiably so, for making the careful judgment that your child does have problems and that appropriate help can be provided.

Teenagers, for their part, are particularly concerned about how they see themselves and how others will judge them. They may think that something is truly wrong with them if they are seen by a mental health professional—"I may have problems, but I am not sick." And they are likely to have as many misconceptions about therapy as their parents. Also, they may have heard cruel jokes about people being "crazy" or "retarded" if seen by a therapist. Their overriding concern, however, is whether their peers will find out (and, unfortunately, other children are simply not tactful). The slight risks involved have to be balanced against discovering ways to overcome the problems being presented and the potential blocks to their growth and development.

WHAT TO SAY TO YOUR TEENAGER

When you have decided to seek therapy for your teenager, explain to him or her that a therapist sees many young adults about specific problems. It does not mean that they are "crazy." In fact, many people find it quite useful to have someone to talk to about their personal secrets or problems or anxieties. You may want to add that this matter will be kept within the family. You also may want to say that you will be there, if needed, and are committed to seeing that he or she will be getting the best help available. More than likely, an older teen will want no part of parental interference in the therapeutic relationship, but that will depend on the family and on the therapist's approach to the problems.

In many circumstances, parents are pressured from the school or other agencies involved with their teenager to seek counseling or therapy. By this time, the difficulties of the teenager have escalated to the point of being a severe disruption to others. When this occurs, it is best to talk about the need for therapy as a team approach to overcoming problems, that is, only people directly involved with your teenager will be working together for his or her betterment. In this way, your child will not feel betrayed if the teacher or nurse is contacted by the therapist. However, therapy is confidential, and it is up to you as a parent to decide if it will be worthwhile for other people to know about the treatment plans.

Actually, children (even older teens) expect adults to know about their problems and are not surprised when many adults are concerned about their progress. Also, they expect, just like in a doctor's office, that their parents will be asking many questions of their therapist. The therapist, in turn, has to judge what and how much to tell the parents about the child's problems. Although confidentiality is crucial, the therapist gives much consideration to what, if anything, will be discussed with a teacher or others involved in the teen's care.

Helping Your Teenager Accept Treatment

What happens if, after you have reviewed all these possible concerns, your teen is still balking at the prospect of therapy? One effective way is to insist on treatment but to leave the scheduling or at least choosing the day of the appointment up to the teenager. Offering the teenager some control usually goes a long way! Of course, you must give your teen a time frame (for example, making a decision within a certain number of days) and allude to the fact that you will make the decision if he or she has not done so before that period of time expires. With this strategy, your teen will most assuredly want the control of at least choosing a preferable day, if not making the actual appointment. Most likely, though, you should expect to wait to the very last minute!

If this strategy fails, you may want to enlist the help of other family members, relatives, or friends, even to the extent of asking them to come to the first session. If your efforts are still not succeeding, you may want to schedule an appointment for yourself with the specific agenda of discussing other methods of getting your teenager into treatment. By expanding your own problem-solving strategies, you have already begun the process of change within your family.

FINDING THE RIGHT THERAPIST

Once the decision has been made to seek treatment, the next job is finding a suitable therapist. For many reasons, this task can be painstaking. Often, when looking for a doctor, you just ask a friend. But in this case, you may not want a friend or relative to know that you will be taking your adolescent to a therapist or counselor. You may have some misgivings or feel embarrassed. As is often the case, this leaves many parents in a quandary, and they seek the first person they can find. Also, parents who are otherwise good shoppers are hesitant to shop around for a therapist; therefore, they may not find a good match for their teen.

In seeking a suitable match for your child, you have the right to ask questions. Most mental health professionals do want to help you in any way they can. The more particular you are in your choice, ultimately the more satisfied you will be with the outcome. Ideally, you want a therapist who is both competent and concerned about your needs, who is knowledgeable, as well as warm and caring. You should feel a rapport with the therapist in your question and answer process.

In the case of referring your teenager, you will want to know if the therapist is comfortable working with teenagers and whether he or she is seeing teens with similar problems. You also want to know whether the therapist wants to have regular contact with you besides having individual sessions with your child. This latter fact is important to begin setting the guidelines for confidentiality and for expectations of parental involvement. Some therapists prefer seeing the child alone, while others may only want to see the entire family. Most will work with the parents to establish guidelines in their homes and to discover more effective techniques for communication and discipline. Conjointly, they may also assist teenagers to express themselves more appropriately and to problem-solve more adaptively.

PROFESSIONAL DIFFERENCES IN THERAPISTS

Therapists vary in their backgrounds, philosophies, and skills. Some are new to the field, and some have been in practice for many years. Some may specialize in certain disorders, whereas others may focus on a particular age group. Fees also vary, as does the length of time for anticipated change.

In today's environment of managed care, often it is your insurance company that will limit your choices of a therapist and the length of treatment. It is up to you to weigh these differences and to decide what is right for you, your child's problems, and your budget. It is better to be an educated consumer than to be a dissatisfied parent after many months or years of frustration.

As with other professionals, therapists differ in many ways. Licensed mental health professionals include psychiatrists, psychologists, social workers, and psychiatric nurses. Many states have certified counselors who specialize in various pursuits, such as marriage and family problems, or specific therapists, such as pastoral counselors. Their approaches to treatment may be very similar or vastly different. It is best to try to clarify in your mind their particular therapeutic styles over the telephone or at your first appointment.

It is always best to find someone who is licensed in his or her field. To be a member of a regulated profession has many advantages to you and your child. It means that the therapist has received adequate training and supervision and has demonstrated an expertise of psychotherapy. This is likely to include much supervised experience and national certification, as well as proof of completing medical or graduate school.

Licensed therapists are legally bound to work within the professional ethics and standards of their chosen profession. They also have to continue receiving up-to-date education and are legally accountable to their licensing boards. These guidelines provide important protection for you and should be weighed heavily when deciding on an appropriate therapist for your child.

PARENTS' FEELINGS AND REACTIONS

There are common similarities among parents that are beset by a depressed teenager. The prominent characteristic is a feeling of being overwhelmed.

This condition of feeling strained and helpless to come up with a solution is usually the result of many unsuccessful attempts at trying to talk, support, threaten, and punish a troubled youth.

Parents often shudder at the thought or suggestion of seeking professional help for their teenager. A decision to go outside the family for help only increases their sense of frustration and undercuts their competence. When preparing to make contact with a mental health professional, parents are usually feeling very sensitive, somewhat embarrassed, and highly fearful of what they will hear. These feelings need to be addressed and acknowledged by both the family members and the counselor.

INDIVIDUAL THERAPY

In individual therapy, it is the depressed teenager who meets alone with the therapist. Parents will often meet conjointly with the therapist, but the focus is on the teen. Individual therapy differs according to the theoretical beliefs of the therapist and the therapist's own personality and style.

Two major schools of thought in the therapeutic community are the psychodynamic approach and the cognitive-behavioral approach. Psychodynamic therapists see teenage problems as arising from internal struggles and, thus, focus inward, helping the teen gain insight and self-knowledge to resolve conflict. This type of therapy focuses on understanding a teen's feelings layer by layer and tends to be of fairly long duration. Cognitive-behavioral therapists focus on helping the teen interpret his or her environment in a different manner and alter patterns of thinking and behaving. Insight is not paramount in this genre of therapy, and the course of therapy is usually of short to medium duration. Most therapists draw from more than one viewpoint and utilize whatever approaches work!

CONCLUDING COMMENTS

When you choose to find a therapist to work with your family or individually with your teenager, you are primarily hoping for just a little relief from the turmoil and tension that is out of control. You may not be expecting miracles and should not think that everything will dramatically change overnight. The therapist is there to work with you and to assist you in discovering your own resources. Remember, you will be a parent for the rest of your life; the therapist has the privilege of helping you and your family get unstuck only at this particular time. The insights and skills you discover will only be worth the time you invest in the process.

THINGS TO REMEMBER

- Many adolescents believe that therapy is for "crazy" people. It is helpful to explain that therapy is for people who are feeling emotional hurts and pains and need an objective listener.
- There are many therapists willing to help; it is up to you to find a qualified and personable professional.
- Most teens feel a sense of relief after entering therapy and find it useful to be able to share personal feelings and secrets.
- Individual therapists come from a number of different theoretical perspectives, including psychodynamic and cognitive-behavioral.
- Most therapies are helpful to reduce present family tension and to enhance communication.

CHAPTER 12

Seeking Counseling as a Family

LIVING WITH A DEPRESSED TEENAGER

Problems do not occur in isolation. All members within a family will acknowledge that any problem, especially one as severe as depression, impacts on everyone. The following brief example may seem familiar if you feel as though you have a depressed teenager on your hands.

Twelve-year-old Jennifer spoke about the effect of her sister Nicole's depression: "Ever since Nicole started feeling down, I don't have a life! I'm not supposed to invite friends over because it makes her anxious. I'm supposed to be at home at all times when mom and dad are out just 'in case.' Most of all it's just no fun around here anymore because Nicole is usually so irritable that I avoid her." When a teenager is suffering, the entire family has been affected, and every member must start relating with each other a little differently.

In realizing that your whole family feels trapped by the ongoing problems of your teenager, you may want to choose to bring the entire family into therapy. By doing so, the pressures of change are then taken away from the depressed teenager and are apportioned among the various family members. In accepting the need for family treatment, you have acknowledged that problems can be helped by family interactions and can be resolved through learning new ways to talk and behave around one another.

FAMILY THERAPY DEFINED

As the name suggests, *family therapy* is a therapeutic option that engages the entire family in treatment. The depressed adolescent is seen as the "identified patient," but the whole family participates. There are several different schools of family therapy, but, in general, all view the family as a dynamic organism that has distinct sets of rules, patterns of communication, and roles. Family therapy focuses on understanding the unique patterns and roles within the family and altering or enhancing them to allow the family to function better.

Family therapy can enhance family communication and rapport and can help point out both healthy and unhealthy patterns. Often, the teen's depression has placed a heavy weight on the family and, subsequently, has placed pressure on the family's ability to relate to one another. During these sessions, family members can openly express their concerns and feelings to one another in a neutral and safe environment with the help of a professional facilitator.

THE FAMILY'S REACTION TO FAMILY THERAPY

Everyone in the family is bound to experience increased tension and anxiety before a scheduled therapy appointment. Family members may think that too much anger will be produced or that longstanding secrets may be revealed. In many families, there may be unresolved conflicts that have never been dealt with for any number of reasons. Family members might fear that change is at hand and feel uncertain about whether the family will be able to understand and accept the changes.

There will also be some resistance in making the commitment to family therapy. A teenager who is depressed will certainly balk at any intervention. An emotionally distant father may not want to take the time to examine his own feelings or his own contribution to the ongoing problems. Siblings may resist, seeing themselves as "innocent."

However, if you are convinced that family therapy is needed and, in spite of any of your own misgivings, can deal with some minor resistance, then you should have no trouble bringing everyone in for at least the initial session. Your sincerity *will* be heard. You can set up an appointment and insist that all members go without excuses.

One mother of a depressed teen described her family's reaction to the idea of family therapy. "To put it succinctly, their reaction to family therapy was 'No way.' They were supportive of Samantha's individual therapy, but didn't believe that they should be involved. However, when I explained to them that the therapy would be fairly short-term and that it would eventually benefit the whole family, they agreed to give it a try."

BRINGING THE FAMILY INTO COUNSELING

Families enter counseling with shared hope that their pain can be alleviated and soothed. No matter the particular struggle between parents and teenager, parents bring themselves and their family to a counselor's office with the expectation of at least short-term relief and hope for long-term change. During the initial encounter an atmosphere of acceptance is created. It is within this atmosphere that fears can be safely explored without repercussion, and emotional growth can be gained. As one noted family therapist stated, "It's entirely natural for families to feel vulnerable and ill-at-ease at the first session. It's up to the therapist to create a comfortable and trusting atmosphere where all members of the family feel heard and respected."

THE INITIAL STAGES

Families with a depressed teen often share a common emotion—an intense sense of helplessness. Families have tried all sorts of strategies from talking, supporting, and listening empathetically to perhaps threatening and punishing a youngster out of his or her depressed state. Few positive results have emerged. Turning to someone outside of the family can further undermine the family's feelings of desperation and ineptness. The family usually comes into the first therapy session with these burdens. It is up to the clinician to overcome this possible block and to pave the way towards recovery.

Effective change cannot occur when failure is anticipated. When a family is stuck on criticizing, blaming, and punishing one another, there is little energy left for positive gains. Initially, the primary role of the counselor is to buoy the family's confidence that their problems can indeed be resolved.

Once this basis of trust in the therapeutic process is established, change can occur rapidly and eventfully. Everyone involved gains a deeper respect and appreciation for one another.

COMMUNICATING THE TEENAGER'S DEPRESSION

It has been suggested that families with depressed teenagers commonly feel angry, irritated, and helpless. These feelings often surface when confrontation occurs between family members. These feelings are generally shown through intense conflict on the one hand or complete withdrawal and avoidance of one another's feelings on the other. So, if your family is experiencing exasperation and anger, you are not alone.

For some families, though, it is the teenager who has become the receptacle for all the family members' negative feelings. Criticizing and blaming one another become common for families under stress. In this case, either the teenager is blamed for everyone's misery, or one or the other parent is being blamed for his or her lack of involvement with the teen. It is these families who become fixated into a global, negative view that is maintained by the depressed teenager. They continue to confront their inability to help their teenager, and their failure creates additional mood swings as they have to deal with their own frustration. As parents, it is very difficult to notice and acknowledge that you may be blaming your teen for family chaos.

When families are confronted with a teenager who becomes depressed, they may erroneously entangle the reactions to their teenager with his or her self-concept and feelings toward the other family members. This linkup, or association, produces common statements like "If you really loved me, there wouldn't be a need for you to be depressed" or, conversely, "If I was a better parent, you wouldn't be depressed." These self-statements turn into a family proclamation regarding how each member values the other. The emotional contempt within these statements clouds the reality of the situation and stifles the opportunity for strengthened family communication and growth.

Once the family has made the first call to the therapist, the process of disentangling negative thoughts and emotions begins. The call is often the first public statement from the family that they acknowledge the need for outside help.

Problems persist when families refuse to let go of or simply cannot let go of perceiving each other's motives as intentionally hurtful. This is frequently seen in families (a) who cannot forgive either themselves or each other for their behavior; (b) in which intense anger dominates the household; or (c) in which several members are suffering from a mood disturbance. These families cannot activate their own internal resources. They are comfortable with their pain because it creates a common bond. Without it, they fear independence and abandonment.

READINESS FOR CHANGE

Once the family has committed to share their collective pain with a counselor, a collaboration has begun to orient the treatment toward the teenager's problems and toward concerns that have impacted the family. When the family has entered counseling with a depressed teenager, it is often the case that three things have happened to maintain the depression and the family dysfunction. They are that: (a) the parental roles have declined or deteriorated; (b) the hierarchy in the family has been confused; and (c) the teenager is expressing parental grief.

When Parents Need to Strengthen Their Roles

Families function best when parents relate well to each other and function as a team. One reason for "acting out" during adolescence occurs when parents are no longer functioning effectively in these roles. These roles may include giving directions, setting limits, and offering support. When these parental roles are not adequately fulfilled, the initial emphasis during therapy becomes focused on helping parents to become comfortable once again in their active parenting roles. Within this therapeutic framework, the depressed symptoms of the teenager are viewed as a temporary manifestation. By working as a family unit, the problems can be addressed and resolved.

Example: Mark's Family

Mark, 16 years old, had begun to violate his parent's curfew and had become verbally abusive. His grades had plummeted, and his school behavior had deteriorated. His moods swung in cycles, and he constantly complained about not feeling well and needing to stay home from school. In desperation and exasperated with his belligerence, his parents brought him to an outpatient mental health clinic. It was there that their story unraveled and that they were able to share their stress with one another.

It was apparent that Mark's behavior began to deteriorate after his grandmother had become chronically ill and required continuous attention and care. This had taken up much of the parents' extra time and energy. Mark felt angry but guilty for feeling this way. He began to test the limits for his own freedom and to divert his own sadness over the situation. Soon the parents were in a no-win contest of words with him. Punishment seemed of little use.

As the parents began withdrawing even more from Mark due to his misbehavior and agitation, he became increasingly defiant. He also began taking their avoidance of him as a signal that they no longer cared. He began fantasizing and occasionally verbalizing that they would probably be better off without him. This only had the impact of making the parents feel like failures and impotent to change this defeating cycle. When they finally arrived at the outpatient clinic, they were noticeably anxious and sullen.

This example illustrates a family in which a tragic but common development has led both to a change in the family structure and to a reaction to the change. Mark's parents made attempts at straightening out the situation by taking care of the grandmother but felt tired and overwhelmed by the new demands placed on them. The more they felt defeated, the less energy remained to maintain their primary role as parents. In addition, as Mark's fears heightened that he was been ignored by his parents, the more his attention-seeking misbehavior escalated.

By reestablishing their principle role, the parents regained a sense of control over the family.

Restructuring the Family Hierarchy

Symptoms of depression can emerge as a result of placing a teenager in a caregiving role. This role of taking over for a parent who has become dysfunctional places the teenager in a position for which he or she has not been adequately prepared. The teenager is pushed into a precocious role at that time to assist the parent(s). This signals confusion over who really is in charge of the family. This child has now taken over for the parent. However, the undue stress that is the usual result turns into depressive symptoms.

In such situations, the therapist will focus on how to reestablish the parents as "in charge." This, undoubtedly, becomes a delicate process because the family is already feeling vulnerable and the idea of change can be very frightening!

Families that find themselves in this situation have usually been through some kind of crisis such as separation or divorce, illness or death, loss or transfer of a job. Due to the crisis, the parent may inadvertently solicit help from the teenager instead of finding help from other adults. All of a sudden, the teenager is no longer a child because he or she has to become a confidant, baby-sitter, housekeeper, or parent to younger siblings. Their link to other teenagers has been broken.

This "parentified child" then begins to act in a pseudomature manner that may seem productive for awhile but that often results in the teenager displaying inappropriate behaviors, and interacting with the older peer.

Example

One couple saw this happening with their adolescent son when they moved overseas. Sixteen-year-old John was attending a local school and so was learning his host country's language more rapidly than either of his parents. His parents began to rely on John for almost all the interactions with local agencies, neighbors, and so forth. At first, John felt proud and helpful, but soon he began to demonstrate resentment and then depression for having to be the "voice" for his family. When the parents consulted with a family therapist, the dynamic was pointed out, and the parents became more aggressive in learning the language and in staying within their defined roles as parents.

When faced with changing this structure in therapy, the family may initially be hesitant to lose what they may perceive as an increase in intimacy. They fail to see the costs, though, and often overlook the teenager's depression as a by-product of this inappropriate closeness. It is only when boundaries can be reestablished that a truer closeness between parent and child can result.

Example: Amy's Family

Amy was 14 years old when she came with her family for counseling. Amy had become increasingly out of control, was suspected of drug usage, had failed all her classes during the past semester, and was hanging out with an older crowd. She appeared older than her stated age; in fact, the therapist had to continually remind herself of Amy's age.

Through the sessions, it was discovered that the mother had become severely depressed, quit her job, and had been hospitalized for a brief time. Before these events, the parents had been arguing bitterly, and the father had threatened divorce on several occasions. In response to her mother's incapacity, Amy began gradually to assume all her roles, including taking care of the house and cooking meals. She had initially withdrawn from her own friends and school activities.

As she appeared more and more competent on the surface, the parents (especially the father) began to depend on her more. However, this only compounded the problem because Amy began seeing herself as an adult and demanding adult privileges. Soon, she started testing the limits of her curfew and began dating older boys. This eventually led to her fleeing from her household and becoming lost in an age gap.

Due to the bitterness between Amy's parents and her mother's own depression, Amy was thrust into a role that she initially accepted, but in which she soon felt trapped. Her reactions to the unnecessary burden of taking over her mother's role and withdrawing from her peers placed her in an untenable position. She clearly was not ready to assume these adult roles and felt pressured into continuing them as the father showered her with praise. Her pseudomaturity quickly became an outlet for escape. She needed not only relief from her responsibilities, but also a way to rid herself of unacceptable angry feelings at her parents.

The counselor in this situation did not buy into the family's fear that they could not survive the attempt at making the changes for a healthier family dynamic. The counselor focused primarily on each family member's role. The need was to examine Amy's symptoms separate from her and her family's relationship.

In this case, it was important to reframe Amy's defiant behavior as a means to get her mother back into a parental role. The father reduced his need to view Amy as a peer and confidant and, thus, helped unburden her with trying to replace the mother. It was also important to point out that Amy had become the caretaker for both parents. This prompted the mother to restore her own status as guardian, which emphasized a more appropriate hierarchy for the family. Within this case, Amy's depression and subsequent symptoms were viewed as a metaphor of the family's structural problems.

Families Unable to Share on an Emotional Level

It is often the case that families develop communication problems following the loss of a loved one, whether the loss be through separation or death. Teenagers, in particular, are sensitive to their parents' pain. During those times, teens may begin to show symptoms of depression as a way to protect and distract their parents. By becoming depressed, they are offering their parents a way out from feeling miserable.

Rarely do families enter counseling during the actual time of bereavement. Reactions to the loss may be delayed. Many times, a teenager's depression is related to the past grief. It is not uncommon that the depression is a reflection of what the parents had felt or experienced at the time of the loss. Therefore, the depression can be viewed as a pervasive problem for the family to resolve, not merely something that is occurring to one member (i.e., the teenager).

Once in counseling, the initial goal is to ventilate these pent-up emotions and to clearly express the feelings of loss and grief. This process allows the family to share their pain with one another in a supportive and protective environment, as well as to gain control over these emotions.

If the teenager's depression was partly a by-product of distracting the parents' pain, counseling can be used to help the parents gain comfort in expressing their unpleasant feelings. When this is accomplished, the teenager can be relieved of this burden. The parents also discover how to resolve and work through painful episodes. The process then becomes an excellent instructional platform because the parents are given the chance to model more appropriate expression of loss for the future.

Example: Tom's Family

Seventeen-year-old Tom was brought into counseling by his mother. "I don't know what to do with him," she stated in frustration. "His grades are fast deteriorating, he's alienating his friends, and he's always complaining about aches and pains and other maladies." A physical examination had revealed that he was healthy.

During their first counseling session, it was discovered that the father had died 10 years ago and that the mother "had to" work two jobs in order to support herself and Tom. This reduced time not only with her son, but also with her social sphere. She no longer had time to meet new people. Because Tom was bright and mostly responsible, he had the opportunity to gain scholarships for college. However, his recent deterioration was limiting his possibilities. The mother became exasperated and angry over this matter, but that only led to increasing frustration in trying to get Tom to "snap out of his doldrums."

This case illustrates several issues. First, it is common for symptoms to appear when separation is imminent. Second, depressive symptoms occur frequently in families that have previously experienced unacknowledged loss. In the example, the mother threw herself into work, which limited her to only superficial contact with others. Tom's behavior paralleled his mother's. (In this situation, he attempted to isolate himself by jeopardizing his chance to leave home.) If he were to leave, the mother would have to confront her loneliness and possibly relive her husband's passing. Tom, in failing to continue in school, remained a trusted son and continued to allow the mother her role as mother and caretaker. His symptoms, however, were self-defeating and served little value for a productive, healthy future.

In beginning a counseling relationship, this mother and son needed help in resolving their previous loss before being able to overcome the present problems. The focus of the sessions moved from the son's present symptoms to the mother's need to come to terms with her loneliness and self-imposed isolation. This provided her with permission to seek solace and companionship from other adults and allowed her son the opportunity to maximize his own potential.

By taking the time to share past feelings, Tom and his mother could now examine their present circumstances. By approaching this once taboo topic openly and without fear, there was less need for Tom's symptoms to play a function within the family.

In this case, their feelings toward the father's death were relatively easy to access. This allowed for a quicker transition from Tom's depressive symptoms to a sharing of emotions. Some families may find this difficult because the symptoms are so entrenched in their daily interactions. However, it becomes imperative for parents to resolve their past issues to unburden the teenager. In situations like Tom's, where loss and grief were shared, counseling becomes a time when the parent can help the child work through the trauma by becoming a role model.

SUMMARY

The counseling sessions and therapeutic strategies discussed in this chapter represent just a few of the common approaches used in assisting families with depressed teenagers. Family sessions provide a safe and structured arena to explore family functioning and the willingness for change. Each family has its own perspective, expectations, and resources to give to the counselor upon seeking advice about how to overcome their distress. The counselor accepts this challenge and makes his or her best attempt to help the family.

While this chapter focused on family treatment, there also must be an acknowledgment that some cases need additional treatment in the form of individual or group therapies or, in some cases, medication. Depression that has persisted for a long time is bound to influence the natural growth and development of a teenager. Because of these delays, the teen's self-esteem is likely to suffer; thus, working individually or within a group becomes an important ingredient toward overcoming emotional deficits. Also, working with another person or with peers provides valuable experiences for the teen to gain much needed social skills. When medication is used as a supplement to treatment, it is used not only to relieve symptoms but also to make the teenager more available for these other therapies.

Family therapy is essential through this process in order to make home life more tolerable. It places a value on each family member and intervenes at a level of enhanced communication. It assumes that, by working together, each member will be better able to address his or her own needs, as well as to support the others in their pursuit of health. The counselor then becomes a temporary assistant in this process toward growth. The counselor's goal is to quickly become "unemployed" by the family in order that the family can use their own resources for healthy change.

THINGS TO REMEMBER

- Family counseling can help improve communication among all family members.

- A teen reluctant to enter individual treatment may readily engage in family counseling because he or she feels less in the spotlight.
- Most families feel exhausted and powerless when entering therapy.
- Family counseling can offer parents the tools to further negotiate problems successfully.
- Family counseling acknowledges not only that each family is unique, but that the answers for productive change lie within the resources of the family and not solely within the practitioner.
- Three primary focuses of family counseling include strengthening parental roles, restructuring family hierarchies, and improving communication about emotionally laden issues.

CHAPTER 13

The Use of Medication in Treating Teenage Depression

Jeff

Jeff, 13 years of age, was referred to a child psychiatrist after his school expressed concerns He was constantly fidgety and disruptive in class and was seen as emotionless. He also made references to feeling hopeless and self-destructive. At home, his parents mentioned that he was ungovernable, and, on at least one occasion, he had run away for two weeks. Substance abuse was suspected but was denied and never proved. Prior attempts at therapy had failed, but now he seemed to admit that he needed help.

Upon presenting for an evaluation, Jeff seemed insecure, anxious, and depressed, with a limited capacity to express his emotions. He appeared to rely on actions to express his frustrations, anger, and sadness. Once on medication, his uncaring facade and irritability diminished, but much therapeutic work was still needed for him and his family.

Kimberly

Kimberly was 16 years old when she was admitted into a psychiatric hospital after persistent running away, and a suicidal attempt consisting of swallowing 17 of her mother's diet pills. Her parents were unable to control her behavior. Prior assessments described her as possessing low self-esteem, as being socially isolated and vulnerable to depression, and as having little control over her impulses. Her previous trials on medications were reviewed by the consulting psychiatrist who thought that a different kind of antidepressant might be warranted. After several weeks on this new medication, Kimberly seemed more amenable to treatment alternatives and was no longer experiencing suicidal thoughts.

WHEN TO CONSIDER MEDICATION

Although medication has been used to treat emotional problems in children and adolescents for many years, only recently has considerable attention been paid to pediatric psychopharmacology. This renewed emphasis has brought pediatricians and child psychiatrists more up-to-date information than ever before on the benefits and risks of prescribing medication to preadult populations. With this knowledge, clinicians can now make purposeful and practical medication interventions that can positively impact on a teenager's depression and lessen the risk of suicide.

Medications, like all therapeutic interventions, are used to promote optimal development and maturation by removing certain obstacles that are blocking healthy, adaptive functioning. However, they should be viewed as only one part of a troubled teenager's overall treatment plan that ideally incorporates a multimodal approach with assistance from doctors, therapists, and educators. Drug therapy's main benefit is to assist the teenager in becoming more available and responsive to these other therapeutic approaches.

Medication is used for many forms of adolescent emotional problems, from extreme conditions such as psychosis and severe anxiety reactions to lesser problems such as bed-wetting and sleep disturbance. Probably, the most frequent use of medication during the preadult years is to increase the attention span in those youths who appear restless, excitable, and hyperactive. It has been reported that approximately 750,000 children in this country at any one time are being prescribed psychostimulants (e.g., Ritalin, Cylert, Dexidrine) to improve those symptoms. As depression is becoming more recognized as a major problem to effective adjustment through the teenage years, the use of medication as a therapeutic supplement is on the rise.

WORRYING ABOUT MEDICATION USE

Many parents may worry about placing their children on medications that have been used primarily with adults. They wonder about the message that they may be giving by promoting emotional relief with a pill. After all, as a society, we are trying to deliver the message that drugs are not the way to solve problems and that problems can be solved by other methods. Parents might say, "Wouldn't it be better for my son to learn these methods rather than to rely on drugs? Will he get the message that drugs are always to be depended upon to relieve stress?!"

It is very important that adults be aware of the messages they convey to youngsters. However, in this instance, the concern is with teenagers whose underlying depression is impairing their everyday functioning. Due to their sadness, they can no longer concentrate, have lost interest in friends and activities, and have become withdrawn and irritable. If medication offers the possibility of a quicker and fuller recovery, it is incumbent upon parents and professional caregivers to weigh the benefits against the possible risks.

If a medication trial seems appropriate, it becomes the doctor's responsibility to educate both the teenager and the parent regarding the use of antidepressants. Such ongoing discussions should include (a) identifying target symptoms, (b) describing how the medicine works, (c) how long to expect to use it, and (d) how medicine use differs from drug use in the conventional sense. It is frequently reassuring for most families to know, for example, that antidepressants are not stimulants. They help alleviate depression but do not produce a "high." They do not cause physical dependence and are not addictive. Prescribed medication is often designed to be taken on a time-limited basis.

The use of antidepressant medication does not preclude counseling. Individual, family, or group therapy may be recommended. These sessions should be directed toward the concerns regarding medicine use, as well as toward encouraging more adaptive means to deal with internal and external stress. It is anticipated that these new ways of learning to manage feelings and concerns through the therapies will continue, even after the medication is discontinued.

GENERAL GUIDELINES TO USING MEDICATION

Rarely do adolescents refer themselves for counseling, and even more rarely do teenagers seek medication for symptom relief. They are certainly not the most willing of patients. They may think that pills are only for "crazy people" or that the suggestion of medication means that they must be "mentally ill." Also, they worry about what their friends might think of them. Additionally, parents, teachers, and counselors are rightly suspicious of drug interventions and are rarely in favor of its use before other sources of therapeutic and educational assistance have been tried.

In order for medication to make an impact, though, the attitude toward medication and cooperation with the doctor play an important role. Adults involved directly in the teen's life, that is, parents, teachers, and counselors, are essential sources of information to the doctor about the teen's functioning. Their willingness to make the necessary observations and to ensure that the teenager remains on the prescribed dosage are keys to success.

Teenagers with unreliable people behind them (who do not observe, administer, and monitor the medication) will undoubtedly not benefit from any type of medication treatment. Parents need to be educated as to the likely benefits, side effects, and, most importantly, toxicity levels with medication, especially when suicide attempts are a concern.

In order to make an appropriate selection of medication, your physician will consider your teenager's particular symptoms, current health, medical and family history, and present versus past functioning. Because the criteria for selecting medications for adolescents are not always clearly defined, your physician is likely to select only those medications with proven results.

If the usual brands and dosages administered do not produce beneficial results, your doctor may try other medications. Rapidly becoming available are many new antidepressant medications that promise quicker and safer relief; thus, it may be prudent to switch to these newer brands if no positive effects are seen from the older medications. Generally, doctors begin with a low dosage and raise the dosage gradually until therapeutic effects are observed or until the onset of any side effects. Doctors do try to establish an acceptable balance between wanted and unwanted medication-induced effects.

PROBLEMS WITH SIDE EFFECTS

Teenagers are especially sensitive about their bodies and how they work. They can quite easily become suspicious and sometimes frightened if there is a sudden change in their regular body functions. Such side effects as dry mouth or frequent urination are not uncommon. The feelings related to the annoyances of side effects may interfere with a teen's compliance in taking the medication. This is why it is incumbent on both parent and physician to have teenagers involved in the entire process. This includes hearing and understanding the teen's concerns and possible complaints about the medication's side effects.

Even though medications do work and, in some cases, produce pronounced "positive" effects, health and mental health professionals are cautious to prescribe them. Parents are rightly concerned, especially after hearing about occasional adverse reactions from medications. However, many of these stories have been greatly exaggerated. In truth, the efficacy of medication in treatment of children and adolescents is by no means definitive and remains a controversial subject. Although there is reason to believe that antidepressant medication helps alleviate depression in adolescents, the jury is still out on whether this should be the first line of action.

CONCERNS EXPRESSED BY TEENAGERS ON MEDICATION

As mentioned, teenagers become very concerned about taking medications from doctors, particularly if it has to do with their mental state. They worry about how "sick" they really are. If they must take the medication during the school day, they worry about how others at school will view them and whether they will be ridiculed by peers. They also worry that medication will change their personality.

Most physicians working with adolescents understand that teenagers may be embarrassed at having to do anything different. Teens may balk at being placed on special diets, at having to attend special classes, and certainly at taking medication. The problem can be compounded by a lack of understanding by peers or school staff.

Prior to any use of medicine with a teenager, the doctor needs to discuss these predictable concerns common to all teenagers. Included in such a conversation should be the understanding that medicine is only one form of treatment that can help the teen become more at ease with himself or herself. The choice of medicine is guided by the symptoms present and is not a measure of the teen's character or degree of illness.

Before prescribing regular medication to be taken at school, the parent and the doctor will want to know how it will actually be dispensed and monitored. It is common to find schools having inadequate or nonconfidential mechanisms for taking care of these matters. It becomes imperative for parents to discuss these possible pitfalls with the school nurse in advance.

It is also essential to ask the teenager about specific concerns of taking medication at school. Parents can then correct any misconceptions and can offer help in negotiating ways of handling sensitive issues. Sometimes a doctor can provide an alternative medication or medication schedule that would help avoid potential embarrassment, such as taking time-released medications that may only have to be taken in the morning.

MONITORING THE MEDICATION

The duration of medication treatment for a depressed teenager depends on many factors: (a) the age of the teenager, (b) the type of antidepressant being used, and (c) the uniqueness of the situation. There are several standard guidelines that are generally used, for example, whether there has been a noticeable improvement within four weeks of beginning an adequate medication trial. If the teenager has not responded, the doctor would probably switch to another type of antidepressant.

After establishing a therapeutic response to the medication (the teenager and/or parents report beneficial effects and symptom relief), the anticipated length of stay on the medication is usually six to nine months. Generally speaking, the teenager should not be placed on the medication for more than a year without at least a one- or two- month medicine-free trial. These "drug holidays" are essential to reevaluate the continuing need for medication.

Teenagers need to be seen by the prescribing physician at frequent intervals during the beginning of their medication trial. This should occur every couple of weeks, or even more frequently, with close communication occurring between the teenager, parent, and doctor. Parents should not hesitate to call the doctor during this crucial time period if questions arise or if parents need further clarification. This communication process is essential for maximum benefit to result.

Once the physician is satisfied with an adequate dosage that appears suitable in obtaining the desired outcome, he or she can begin seeing the teenager less frequently, perhaps on a monthly basis. This monitoring of the maintenance dosage allows for periodic reevaluations of the effectiveness of the medication and reviews of any problems. During this time, feedback should be gained from other people involved in the care of the teenager, such as teachers, therapists, or other physicians. This feedback is important to ensure that all factors are being considered when the time approaches to discontinue the medication. When discontinuing the antidepressant, it should be done gradually because an abrupt ending can cause other effects like insomnia, increased anxiety, or an upset stomach.

Teenagers also need to have regular laboratory tests completed when they are placed on medication. These chemistry screenings will occur usually before and after three months of being on the medication and after every six-month interval. Because there is a concern of cardiovascular side effects when placed on certain antidepressants, repeat EKGs are sometimes ordered. Also, during a drug maintenance program, it becomes helpful to have accurate records of weight, height, and other physical changes that the teenager may be experiencing during this period.

THE USE OF ANTIDEPRESSANTS

Although antidepressant drugs are used most often for serious depression, they have also been found helpful for milder forms of depression and to relieve depressive symptoms of other disorders. They have been used to relieve symptoms of anxiety, such as dizziness, rapid heartbeat, and panic disorders. These medications are not stimulants that attempt to make the person feel better than he or she would normally; rather they help the person feel about the same way before the onset of depression.

The use of tricyclic antidepressants (Imipramine®, Desipramine®, and Amitriptyline®) for depression in teenage populations has grown quickly during the past decade. Traditionally, these types of antidepressants have been used with rapid beneficial effects for such conditions as enuresis and hyperactivity. Besides their use in reducing depressed symptoms, they are now being used for other emotional disorders in children and adolescents, sometimes in combination with other medications.

It appears that when these agents are used for depression, it takes several weeks to take effect. Some symptoms disappear relatively early in the treatment (e.g., sleeping and eating may improve), but an enhancement of mood may not be noticed for several weeks. Again, this is a gradual process, and, oftentimes, the teenager will not realize the gains being made.

Another category of antidepressant medication, called *monoamine oxidase inhibitor*® (MAOI), is sometimes used when the symptoms appear unusual or the tricyclic medication does not seem to have made much of an impact. The associated symptoms may be overeating or oversleeping along with intense anxiety attacks. Besides causing some of the same side effects that are seen with tricyclic medication, MAOIs also have the potential for reacting adversely with certain foods, alcohol, and over-the-counter medications. These combinations can cause severe high blood pressure and headaches. Thus, they are generally a second line of defense.

Lithium® is used primarily for bipolar disorders, or what is commonly referred to as manic-depressive illness. It seems most effective in stopping the manic episodes and also appears to decrease the number of depressed episodes.

Lithium is a salt akin to ordinary table salt or sodium chloride. It was discovered by an Australian psychiatrist in 1949 to have a calming effect for patients suffering from uncontrollable mood swings. It has also proven extremely useful in other disorders with mood symptoms. These include certain kinds of depressions, schizophrenic disorders, impulse control and aggressive disorders, personality disorders, and even motor tic disorders.

Depressed persons most likely to respond to Lithium are those that have family members who have been treated for similar problems or whose depression comes and goes rather than remains constant. Lithium can reduce severe manic symptoms in approximately one to two weeks, but it may take as long as several months before the condition is fully stabilized.

Regular blood tests are an essential part of treating someone with lithium. These tests allow the physician to monitor the level of the drug in the blood stream. If too little is being absorbed, no therapeutic effect will take place. Conversely, if too much is being absorbed, a toxic reaction may result. This range between an effective dose and a poisonous one is very small, thus, blood tests are imperative.

Lithium is given to adolescents on occasion when other medications are not effective or when their moods are rapid or violent. These severe mood swings and destructive actions may represent an early form of manic-depressive illness, a depressive disorder, or an aggressive disorder.

PROZAC AND BEYOND

There has been much notoriety about the antidepressant drug Prozac®. First released in December of 1987, Prozac (or fluoxetine) was largely utilized with adult populations. It works by stimulating the activity of serotonin (a chemical neurotransmitter) in the brain. It has long been thought that depression may be caused or maintained by a decrease in the levels of serotonin. Since the main function of fluoxetine is to increase serotonin activity and also to enhance mood and outlook, this provides support for this theorizing.

Many teens and even younger children have been successfully treated with Prozac with relatively few difficulties. Indeed, one of Prozac's interesting properties is its lack of many of the side effects common in other antidepressants, such as blurred vision, dry mouth, weight gain, and cardiac conduction (i.e., heart pumping) effects.

Another positive feature of Prozac is its specific effect on brain chemical transmitters that are possibly involved with obsessive-compulsive disorder (OCD) symptoms. It has been used successfully to treat individuals (adults and children) with OCD and associated depressions. Also and very importantly, Prozac is possibly less lethal in overdose than other antidepressant medications.

Since it is still relatively new, Prozac is usually prescribed only after more established antidepressants, like Imipramine, are administered. One main disadvantage is its cost, which can be as much as 10 times that of older medications. The common dosage is usually 20 mg to 40 mg daily, although up to 80 mg per day is not uncommon.

Prozac may be a drug of choice in the following situations: (a) when there is a family history of a good response to Prozac, (b) when OCD symptoms are present, (c) when there is intolerance to side effects of other antidepressants, (d) when there is inadequate response to other antidepressants, and (e) when there is heart disease that prevents use of other antidepressants. Despite the possible advantages of Prozac and its current popularity, it is not a miracle drug. It does not work for everyone, and it requires certain medical precautions and considerations in its use.

Since the advent of Prozac, many other similarly acting medications (for example, Zoloft® and Paxil®) have become available and are being used judiciously with adolescents. Every day, it seems that a new "wonder drug" has been discovered to do away with emotional setbacks. Even as this book is being written, a new antidepressant is being talked about that impacts on two of the neurotransmitter systems instead of one! These new medications allow physicians to find the optimum drug of choice for depressed symptoms. Remember, though, that each person is different—what works for one person may not work for the next.

THE CAREFUL ADMINISTRATION OF MEDICATION

The best way to encourage proper use of medications is to educate children early and often about medication safety and drug abuse. This education should occur in the home, at school, and within community groups. It is always important to distinguish between properly prescribed and taken medicine and illicitly obtained drugs. The purpose of the medication should be explained carefully, as should the dangers of misuse. Clear expectations should be made by the parent with respect to medicine use and safety.

An overdose of antidepressants is very serious and can be potentially lethal. It requires immediate medical attention, which often means having the stomach pumped in the emergency room. Thus, antidepressants need to be used only in their proper amounts and administered with adult supervision. When used properly and monitored regularly, however, antidepressant medications can be extremely helpful in overcoming depressed states. Teenagers can begin once again to feel good about themselves and to be more accessible to learning and other skill enhancement interventions.

SUMMARY

Although adolescence is certainly a time of major social, emotional, biologic, and physiologic changes, the majority of teens make it through this period without major problems. Those teenagers who do display impairment in functioning—they appear unusually unpredictable or impulsive or pose a danger to themselves or others—need to be evaluated quickly and actively.

Those teens are not experiencing a "natural storm" but are displaying serious signs of dysfunction and may need medication. Even when your teen does not display dramatic symptoms, but is obviously suffering inside, it does not hurt to talk to your physician or a child psychiatrist about possible therapeutic alternatives.

THINGS TO REMEMBER

- Medication is only one part of treatment planning; other therapeutic interventions should not be ignored.
- Medication lessens depressive symptoms so that teenagers can begin talking about their inner feelings and emotions.
- Families need to express all their concerns and have their questions answered before starting their teenager on medications.
- Everyone is unique, so what has proven successful with your neighbor's child may not be the right drug or dosage for your teen. The prescribing physician will work to find the right medication and dosage.
- It generally takes three to six weeks to see the effects of antidepressants, though some teens report more immediate improvement.
- Side effects are a reality for many medications. Make sure you review possible side effects with your doctor so you can continue to talk with your teen about his or her concerns.
- Communicating with everyone involved with your teenager is very important to gauge the effectiveness of the medication.
- Antidepressants are not addictive, but they are powerful substances that must be carefully administered and monitored by caring and responsible adults!
- Newer medications are always coming to the marketplace, so ask your doctor about their differing effects.

CHAPTER 14

When Considering Hospitalization for Your Teenager

June

June, aged 13 years, was taken by her mother to the emergency services of a local children's hospital. Her mother reported to the attending nurse that June had been refusing to get up from bed for the past several mornings, had been making vague complaints about her body, and had been missing school. She also related to the nurse that June had seemed unusually apathetic and lethargic and noted a decrease in her appetite. "This is not the June I knew last year!" her mother exclaimed.

June appeared to the medical staff as being unkempt, despondent, and tearful. She only spoke in brief statements, mostly of anger towards her mother for bringing her to the hospital. After a brief physical exam that found nothing wrong, the primary physician conferred with the psychiatrist-on-call to assess the possibility of depression or the onset of some other emotional disturbance.

Based on a thorough clinical interview with June and her mother, and a behavior checklist that displayed many areas of June's distress, a determination was made and agreed upon by the mother to admit June into the hospital for her own safety and further evaluation.

153

James

James, aged 15 years, was already engaged in individual counseling with a psychologist. His initial problems had revolved around school failure, poor peer relations, and being noncompliant at home. Prior to a scheduled session, his mother phoned the counselor in a panic stating, "James came home from school really wound up and angry; he started threatening to hurt himself and his younger brothers!" Although his mother was not clear what had precipitated the outburst, James was being verbally abusive towards her and had even lit a small fire in one of the trash cans in the house. The mother was directed by James's therapist to bring him and the entire family immediately to the therapist's office for an emergency family session.

At the meeting, although James was still irritable, he was able to say what had made him so upset and was able to apologize for his actions and to think about how else he could have handled his distress. Although the therapist had alerted the admissions coordinator at a psychiatric unit that she was considering hospitalizing James, it was decided during the family session that the parents could negotiate an around-the-clock observation of James and that hospitalization could be bypassed at this time.

It was made clear that it would be available if such a situation reoccurred or if James was not as willing to discuss his emotions. The therapist indicated to the parents that she would be on-call for them during the next several days. She reminded James that his next regular appointment would be a time for continuing the discussion about his outbursts and the possible consequences of his actions.

KEEPING YOUR TEENAGER SAFE

The use of psychiatric inpatient units in general hospitals and free-standing psychiatric hospitals are seen as crucial links to mental health treatment. This is especially true for teenagers who have become severely incapacitated or disruptive and a danger to themselves or others. In fact, the number of youths between the ages of 10 and 19 in this country admitted to psychiatric inpatient care rose approximately 50 percent by the end of the 1980s according to national health statistics. There had been upwards of 200,000 teenagers discharged from hospitals during that time period when the population of that age group had in fact been shrinking! For the 1990s, these psychiatric hospitalizations seem to be leveling off due to the use of alternative treatment options, such as partial hospitalization programs or day hospitals.

Mental health professionals have viewed the rise of teenage admissions to psychiatric wards as a byproduct of trends that converged during the 1980s and 1990s. Family turmoil, such as divorce, remarriage, frequent relocation, and two-career families, without the nearby support of relatives have made it difficult to deal and cope with troubled teenagers. Psychiatric treatment in general has lost some mystery as mental health professionals and hospitals have become more visible to the public. At the same time, many insurance benefits favor inpatient care in their policies, making it actually less expensive (out of the family's pocket) to send a child to a hospital rather than to an outpatient therapist.

As the opening examples illustrate, the need for a more secure and structured setting for teenagers can take on a variety of forms. For June, who had been a bright and cheerful young girl, the suddenness and severity of her depressive symptoms called for very thorough physical and psychological evaluations that only a comprehensive and safe inpatient unit could provide. In that case, the mother, who was single, was also overwhelmed with her own problems and could neither offer immediate support nor call on family or friends to help.

In contrast, James's parents, although visibly upset and worried about his and the family's safety, were able to mobilize their own resources in a final effort to avoid hospitalization. In these two very different situations, the input received and the condition of the familial support were the deciding factors in making the most informed decisions.

PRIMARY PURPOSES OF HOSPITALIZATION

The placement of teenagers in psychiatric hospitals is not a way to relieve stress or to save a marriage, although many parents would contend that the break from their difficult teenager is well deserved and appreciated. The primary goals of the hospitalization should be for assessment and treatment when a controlled environment is required for safety and cooperation.

Removing teenagers from their everyday world—stresses at school, hanging out with a bad crowd, relationship problems—can have an immediate and positive impact. Although an adolescent unit of a general or psychiatric hospital can also be stressful, teenagers usually come from similar sources of trouble. Most have experienced family and school problems, drug usage, running away, and eating or sleeping problems and seem to find comfort in discovering peers that are experiencing similar life conflicts. Many teenagers find solace in the tightly controlled structure of the unit, where there are specific and visible consequences should they lose control.

As opposed to their everyday turmoil before hospitalization, the controlled atmosphere of the psychiatric unit makes daily life very predictable. Each hour of the day is structured; there is a time for school as well as for various therapies. An around-the-clock supportive staff offers not only supervision but also the nurturance and attention that most teenagers need and seek. Instead of continuing in their problematic cycles in which they find few solutions for their problems, depressed teenagers discover problem-solving strategies and gain awareness into their self-defeating behaviors in a safe setting that provides a straightforward routine.

DECIDING WHETHER TO USE
AN INPATIENT SETTING

Short-term psychiatric hospitalization can be one of the strongest and most important vehicles in interrupting the downward spiral of depression in a teenager. Deciding whether or not to hospitalize your teenager, however, can become a complicated matter with many important implications. Some matters are practical, such as your own willingness and beliefs about psychiatric treatment and your particular insurance guidelines and reimbursement. Other considerations are rather vague and out of your control, such as the admission criteria at the hospital and the legal guidelines that govern them. Some common admission criteria include: (a) whether your teenager is in a potentially life-threatening situation (e.g., has he or she already made a suicide gesture?); (b) whether other means of intervention have been tried (e.g., has your teenager already been involved in outpatient treatment?); (c) whether your teenager is ordered into an inpatient setting through social service agencies or the juvenile court (often these agencies rely on hospitals for comprehensive and secured evaluations); and (d) whether your teenager has placed other people in potentially harmful situations (e.g., a teenager becoming destructive and out-of-control in the home).

The final decision of whether to hospitalize a teenager is never clear-cut.

Of paramount consideration are the factors that may be causing your teenager to act out, the actual behaviors that your teen is expressing, the various depressive symptoms that are being experienced, and the supportive network that can help out (other relatives or close friends that are available). In general, the stronger the tension that your teenager is experiencing, and the more destructive and disruptive to the home or school that your teenager has become, the greater the reasons for considering hospitalization.

Due to the high increase in suicide attempts, drug usage, and delinquent activities, an initial "knee jerk" response might be to remove teenagers involved in any of these activities from their immediate environment. It would be hoped that the mere removal from whatever external pressures were influencing the teenager's behavior would at least temporarily protect the teenager from further harm and allow time for treatment to have an impact.

The removal would also allow the family to relax and receive some objective feedback about what was going on with their teenager. Sometimes, it is this brief separation that can have the most beneficial influence in sorting out everyone's thoughts and feelings.

However, even in the most difficult of presenting circumstances, hospitalization can severely disrupt the life of a teenager and provide an unnecessary burden for the rest of his or her life. Thus, each admission must be thoroughly evaluated by both the family and the mental health or legal professionals involved with the teenager.

CRITICISMS OF HOSPITALIZATION

For a long time, there has been resistance from both the general public and from many professionals against exposing teenagers to a psychiatric hospital, especially because it means removing the teenager from more familiar surroundings. Much of this protest surrounds the very important concern that families are often excluded from the treatment intervention. Also, it was argued that stress was added, not removed, when a teenager was placed in a strange environment.

Some critics charged that the methods of containing out-of-control behaviors in a hospital were too severe for teenagers and usually produced more harm than good. Some of the methods pointed to were the use of restraints, isolation, and medication. An additional concern was that when hospitals were used as a first priority, they had the potential for setting the tone for future crisis. The argument was that this would lead to a reliance on outside institutions whenever a crisis occurred.

The critics of hospitalization say it should only be used as a last resort and only in the most severe of circumstances, and then for only days, not weeks or months. They have felt that placing adolescents into a hospital setting only increased the potential for further damaging their already low self-esteem. Removal from their usual life activities also increased the teenager's sense of helplessness and hopelessness because they often would be perceived as being incurable.

Instead of relieving the teenager from outside stressors, the hospitalization would increase their sense of alienation from family and friends!

BEING INVOLVED WITH THE HOSPITAL

Whether or not you have ever had contact with psychiatric hospitals, you will be amazed at how often they differ in their inclusion of the family in their treatment of teenagers. Some exclude the family completely, whereas most view the family as merely an extra source of information. Other less traditional centers of inpatient care use the family as the basis for change, sometimes even to the extent of hospitalizing the whole family. The extent of family participation depends on the hospital philosophy and on the training of the administrators and physicians. Their ideas dictate the kind of treatment course and how welcome the families are as a source for potential change.

If the change process is to be effective, parents must still maintain a sense of control. Removing a teenager has the potential for disempowering the family at a time when they need to feel more empowered. Parents do not want to have it emphasized that they have lost all control of the situation. Instead, parents must become the primary avenue for change. If their authority is taken away by the unit staff, it will only underscore their feelings of ineffectiveness. The nurturance and structure that the hospital unit provides must be given back to the parents.

Scientific research, as well as clinical practice, has indicated that **parental involvement is a vital force for effective treatment intervention to occur**. One such study reported that when parents refused to participate in the program, the overall treatment goals failed 100 percent of the time. In contrast, when parents were active in their involvement, a 64 percent rate of success was observed. Another major study found that when family orientation was the focus in brief hospitalizations, both the parents and the hospitalized teenager perceived the experience as worthwhile with apparent improvements noticed by all.

The absence of parental participation due to hospital preference or parents' resistance leaves the teenager in the precarious situation of spearheading familial change. When change only comes through the teenager, the family is left vulnerable to escalations in the frequency and intensity of future destructive behaviors.

The act of hospitalization should not rescue the teenager or provide a "parentectomy"; instead, it should begin a process of strengthening the family to prevent future crises. The need for parents to feel in charge of their teenager begins at the decision point as to whether hospitalization is actually needed. The admission then becomes the first step towards needed change, not the end goal to a "cure."

PREPARING FOR ADMISSION

Parents and their teenager preparing for hospitalization are likely to experience many mixed and possibly unpleasant feelings. They may be experiencing feelings of guilt and failure. Everyone is bound to be extremely anxious. To some parents, the act of hospitalizing a teenager may represent a failure to meet the emotional needs of their child. For the teenager, the idea of being "locked up" may mean ultimate rejection or punishment for their actions and much anger is likely to ensue.

Unless there has been some time spent in preparing for the admission (which, in most cases, does not happen), the experience may produce many forms of anxious expression. The teenager may be fearing the aspect of meeting new people, having to take unfamiliar tests, or being talked to by "shrinks." Family members are likely to become defensive and may have second thoughts about submitting their child to this experience. This may cause many parents to prematurely remove their teenager from the unit. All these fears are quite normal and need to be addressed with the staff when first admitting the teenager.

Parents need to take the time to discover both the organizational operation of the hospital unit and the policies that govern such things as visiting privileges, phone calls, and weekend passes. It is important that parents *read* all available materials that describe the program to help alleviate their anxieties.

It is also important for parents to ask many questions and to review unclear answers. They should know what would happen if their teenager becomes physically ill or what kinds of procedures would be used to control their child. In bringing these subjects into the open, parents can set the stage for enriched communication between all family members and the treatment team. This increases the likelihood that everyone will be working together instead of against one another during the hospital stay.

Teenagers will have many responses to hospitalization. They are likely to be angry and feel the need to retaliate by rejecting their parents' visits or disrupting family meetings. Other teens might experience "spontaneous recoveries" in an attempt to show their parents that hospitalization is a terrible mistake and, thus, to make them feel guilty. If parents can anticipate some of the reactions from their teenager, they will more likely set the tone that everything is under control and everyone will be much relieved. It is incumbent on the parents and the hospital staff to explore all these possible feelings and reactions as a predictable course of events. It is at that point that further options can be explored for treatment.

ADMISSION TO THE HOSPITAL

When depressed, suicidal, or out-of-control teenagers are brought to a hospital, they will be admitted to the psychiatric unit as a voluntary or involuntary patient. A voluntary admission usually means that the parents acknowledge that their teen has a severe problem and agree to place their child into the hospital for treatment. Voluntary patients have the right to stay as long as necessary and parents, as legal guardians, have the right to sign them out with or without medical advice. However, removing a youth without the doctor's consent may undermine future treatment attempts and gives a very mixed signal to the adolescent. It is understandable, however, that sometimes parents do not like nor agree with the hospital setting and are justified in their wishes to explore alternative placements.

Involuntary admission means that an individual needs help but resists coming to the hospital. Criteria for involuntary hospitalization (also known as "commitment") vary from state to state. Generally speaking, upon examination by qualified professionals (physicians and, in some states, psychologists), individuals must be judged to be in need of treatment and, without such treatment, to be a danger to themselves or others or to be unable to care for their basic needs (eating, grooming, etc.).

Involuntary patients, because of their impaired judgment, must stay in the hospital for a specific period of time for evaluation and treatment. This period of time is determined at a court hearing within the hospital. In many cases, teenagers may be involuntarily committed by their parents signing a petition through the juvenile courts for an evaluation. At other times, the teenager may behave dangerously. The police may be called to bring the teenager to the emergency room where the staff physicians may determine that an involuntary admission is necessary.

COMING ONTO THE UNIT

Once the teenager is signed into the hospital, his or her first contact is likely to be with a registered nurse (RN). The RN will assist parents and their teenager with admission procedures, which include filling out forms and learning about the unit. During this time, parents will learn about their rights and their child's rights and how the treatment program is set up. A brief tour is given that usually includes a schedule of individual and group therapies, family meetings, and privileges.

Parents will be asked to provide a history of their child's emotional problems, family history, physical health, past psychiatric hospitalizations, current medications, and use of drugs and alcohol. Both parents and their teen can provide this information to assist with the admission procedure. Many hospital units are incorporating regularly scheduled meetings with the families for orientation. This seems an even more effective way to allow free discussion about one's reactions to the hospitalization process and to clear up any misunderstandings or misconceptions.

THE TREATMENT TEAM

Once the admission procedure is completed, the teenager will be assigned to a treatment team, which usually consists of a psychiatrist, a psychologist, a social worker, a nurse, and an activity therapist. Oftentimes, there are mental health workers who assist in providing care and who may serve as your child's advocate. Following a psychiatric evaluation, which is usually conducted by the admitting or staff psychiatrist, the treatment team will develop a course of action.

The team approach is helpful because it brings together the observation of the various professionals. Typically, the treatment team will meet once a week (or more often if needed) for patient conferences to discuss the teenager's progress. Treatment may be modified or changed depending on the course of events or recommendations from the team. These modifications will then be discussed with the teenager and, when possible, with family members.

Psychiatrists are directly responsible for the overall treatment and care of the patient during the hospitalization. In addition to coordinating the treatment plan, they may conduct individual or group psychotherapy on the unit, and prescribe any necessary medications. Because they are physicians, they will also direct a complete physical evaluation and order any specialized tests or medical consultations that may be required. Psychiatrists, in most instances, visit their patients on a regular basis.

Psychologists function in many capacities in the hospital setting, working on both medical and psychiatric units. Their primary responsibility is to perform psychological or neuropsychological evaluations and to provide test reports for use by the treatment team. Their findings are often helpful in establishing a diagnosis or in ruling out certain types of emotional disturbances. In addition to psychological testing, they conduct individual, group, or family therapy sessions, as well as provide consultation or supervision to other professional staff.

Social workers are responsible for obtaining a complete social history from the patient and the family. Their knowledge of social support systems is used to help the teenager and the family with plans after discharge from the hospital. Social workers may also provide educational programming, as well as individual, group, or family therapy sessions on the unit.

Psychiatric nurses are responsible for providing round-the-clock continuity of treatment for psychiatric and physical problems. Their role includes intake and admission of new patients, dispensing and evaluating responses to medications, physical management, coordinating team input, and group counseling.

Activity or expressive therapists belong to a profession composed of many different disciplines. They may specialize in occupational and/or recreational therapy or the creative arts therapies, such as music, art, or movement. By providing therapeutic activities that allow for a daily routine, they promote interaction with the staff and with other patients on the unit.

Mental health workers (sometimes called psychiatric technicians) are trained paraprofessionals who assist in the day-to-day activities of inpatient treatment. Their roles include assisting in the admission of new patients, participating with patients in unit activities, providing patient assessments, physical management, and crisis intervention.

METHODS OF TREATMENT

Your teenager's treatment begins immediately after being admitted to the unit. A combination of three basic treatment approaches is generally used: biological, psychological, and milieu.

Biological Treatment

Biological treatment consists of improving the patient's functioning through the use of medications, diet, or physical procedures. Medications are common to psychiatric treatment but are used judiciously. Significant advances have been made in drug research during the past several years. Today's medications are faster acting, have fewer side effects, and are more selective for certain symptoms.

Medications do not cure mental illness; they control it by reducing or eliminating the disabling symptom. Sometimes, their effects are relatively rapid and dramatic. Generally speaking, the amount of time it takes to bring symptoms under control varies from one individual to another. Because every person responds to medication in a unique way, it is sometimes difficult to predict exactly how much any one person will benefit or how long it will take for a medication to produce a beneficial response. The results will emerge often through the doctor's and staff's careful observations during the hospital stay.

Psychological Treatment

Psychological treatment attempts to improve the patient's functioning through the process of individual, group, and/or family psychotherapy. All psychotherapy involves talking and/or activities. The teenager will most likely have regular sessions scheduled with his or her psychiatrist, psychologist, social worker, or nurse. The therapist, through careful and attentive listening, attempts to understand the patient's feelings and situation. By the teenager and therapist working together, a relationship is established that helps the teenager to rebuild trust and to explore his or her reasons for coming into the hospital.

The therapist offers a teenager emotional support and guidance in an effort to discover better coping skills, thereby promoting communication and self-understanding. Besides feeling frightened, teenagers often feel embarrassed, ill-at-ease, and ashamed of their need for hospitalization, at least initially. Therapy can be helpful in managing these uncomfortable feelings and in assisting in the rebuilding process that continues once the teenager leaves the hospital.

Movement therapy and art therapy are both valuable therapies to increase spontaneity and to gain insight and are offered in most hospitals. Certain teens who may not be able to express themselves verbally find movement and art much more powerful ways to express and work through their conflicts.

Milieu Treatment

Milieu treatment focuses on the patient's total environment by providing activities that allow for a daily routine. Through the use of specially designed activities that include exercise, crafts, music, art, leisure counseling, and social outings, patients are encouraged to take responsibility for their own treatment. Creative, recreational, and work-related activities enable teenagers to learn to express their problems in new ways while rebuilding sound social relationships. The goal of the milieu concept is to improve the teen's overall level of functioning by developing more effective ways of coping with everyday problems in living.

THE FAMILY'S ROLE DURING HOSPITALIZATION

The help that family, relatives, and close friends provide goes a long way in normalizing the experience and seeking positive change. Because families of hospitalized teenagers sometimes feel left out during this time, many hospitals have begun to offer family evening groups. Here, they are encouraged to voice concerns, ask questions, and become aware of what other families think and feel. This will help them deal with the many uncomfortable, but common, emotions that arise. Feelings such as shock, guilt, shame, fear, sadness, and anger are not unusual during this stressful period and need to be discussed. It also becomes important to hear from other parents about their specific issues and concerns and how they deal with their teenager's depression.

WHAT HAPPENS AFTER HOSPITALIZATION?

By the time a teenager is ready to leave the hospital, decisions regarding placement will have been made. This responsibility belongs to the psychiatrist, with the aid of the treatment team, whose recommendations to the family are based on three factors: (a) the teenager's overall level of improvement while in the hospital; (b) the amount of supervision and structure necessary in aftercare; and (c) the family's interest in supporting continuing treatment.

If the teenager has responded well to treatment, there will be a reduction in symptoms and improved social functioning. Teenagers who show solid improvement will likely return home to their families. Because the need for structure and supervision is minimal, follow-up psychotherapy and medication will be provided on an outpatient basis. It is important to keep in mind that not all psychiatrists or therapists treat troubled adolescents. Making inquiries before deciding on a therapist may help avoid unnecessary frustration.

For those teenagers who show moderate improvement, additional structure and guidance may be necessary for effective convalescence. Some teenagers may do well returning home, whereas others may benefit from an alternative living arrangement. Participation in a day or partial hospital program may be helpful for those teenagers needing more structure than outpatient settings can provide. A day hospital provides most services that inpatient hospitals provide, but patients stay only during daytime hours. Sometimes it may be necessary to seek support in the form of a residential treatment facility that provides services, either daily or residential, five to seven days a week.

WHAT IS RESIDENTIAL TREATMENT?

Residential treatment programs are intensive, 24-hour care centers that offer an alternative home setting; therapeutic, educational, and vocational training; and professional support staff. They are similar to hospital programs, but they are usually more flexible and less restrictive. They resemble boarding schools, except that therapeutic services play an integral role in the everyday organization.

A wide variety of residential treatment programs exist across the country to serve adolescents with a broad range of social, educational, and emotional problems. These centers are wide-ranging in their treatment philosophies and behavioral goals. Some are long distance, some are in the community. Some include the family in all aspects of treatment, whereas others exclude family participation.

Although on the surface they might seem to be just other institutions, most residential programs aspire to create real-world environments. They try to challenge the teenagers to be more responsible by earning additional freedoms through their own efforts. Most encourage frequent home visits from the start so the teenagers do not feel "put away" and parents do not get the feeling that they have merely separated themselves from their problem.

CONFUSION AND CHALLENGES

Naturally, parents can be confused by all these choices; and when a teenager is ready to return home, new challenges must be faced. Every family has unique ways of reacting to and coping with the stress of post-hospitalization, and parents will want to know that their actions are in the child's best interests.

It is important to recognize the teenager's need for respect, caring, and personal dignity. An atmosphere of acceptance, kindness, and understanding will be most helpful in promoting a good recovery. The teenager will also make a better adjustment if parents encourage as much independence as possible. Being overprotective might cause the teenager to become too dependent on the family, resulting in a lack of self-responsibility.

Families should make every effort to support their teenager in continuing treatment. This includes taking medication regularly, reporting side effects, keeping psychotherapy appointments, and staying in regular contact with the psychiatrist and outpatient therapist should changes in the teenager's condition occur.

QUESTIONS FROM TEENS

It is very natural for adolescents to have a myriad of concerns and questions regarding the hospital and the transition back to their "regular" life post-hospitalization. A typical question asked during the hospital stay and discharge is "What should I tell the kids at school about where I have been?" Teens *will* ask this of classmates who seem to have disappeared for a few days or weeks. Kids are curious, and rightly so. The staff at the hospital can be invaluable in helping parents answer questions such as these—they have experienced the comings and goings of many teens. Use this resource! One way teens can answer this question is by stating that they had a "personal problem" they had to take care of or were "out sick." Both answers are true but do not force the teen to reveal more than he or she is comfortable revealing.

WHAT YOU CAN DO

Overall, the experience of having a teenager hospitalized can be frightening and difficult. Strong and unpleasant associations and emotions occur that may leave you, the parents, and your family feeling overwhelmed and helpless.

Several things may be helpful in regaining a sense of security:

1. Your family should discuss the situation openly and honestly with all members if possible. Try to decide how much responsibility you are able to assume, based on a realistic assessment of strengths and limitations, in taking care of your teenager at home. Any questions you have can be directed to the hospital social worker, who is generally responsible for discharge planning.

2. Most families do not have the background or experience to deal with mental health professionals. Families often feel awkward and intimidated when talking with a psychiatrist for the first time. You need not feel this

way. Do not be afraid to discuss whatever is on your mind. It is important to ask questions about anything you do not understand.

3. You are facing one of life's most complex situations. It is not unusual for family members to feel a heavy burden of guilt, caused by a need to blame. But—you must not blame yourself. Feeling guilty will not help you in coping during this difficult time.

4. You might want to consider getting some help in the form of counseling for yourselves or becoming involved in a family support group, such as The Alliance for the Mentally Ill or National Mental Health Association. Many families find they get their best support from each other, because no one else can be as understanding as other parents.

THINGS TO REMEMBER

- Hospitalization is a crucial and invaluable link for teens who have become a danger to themselves or others.
- The primary goals of hospitalization are assessment and treatment when a controlled environment is needed for safety and cooperation.
- Hospitals vary greatly in their inclusion of families in treatment—ask about a particular hospital's philosophy.
- Upon admission, teens will have pressing concerns about pragmatics such as visitation privileges, phone calls, week-end passes, and so on. Take the time to help them get answers to these questions.
- It is normal for teens to feel some anger toward parents when entering a hospital—anticipate this!
- Psychiatric hospitals and psychiatric units have a cast of professionals who work together on a treatment team to provide comprehensive services to you and your family. It is up to you to ask questions of these people and to help them understand your teen.
- A successful transition out of the hospital is just as important as the admission process. Take the time to answer all questions from your teenager, as well as other family members. Make sure the support does not end at the hospital exit.
- Parents considering residential placement for their children are bound to have mixed emotions—you are not alone!

- Most hospitalizations or placements incorporate a formal process of gradually transitioning youth out of their highly structured program into a lesser restrictive environment of home or alternative care.
- Returning home does not mean that problems all have been solved; it means the possibility of a new beginning in which everyone in the family is taking responsibility for working on solutions for everyday living.

Concluding
Remarks

What is behind the sadness and anger that flash across the faces of teenagers? By now, you have had the opportunity to reflect on your own situations and it is hoped, have gained some new information and insights about teenage depression. Remember, it has only been during the past 15 years or so that mental health professionals have concurred that serious mood disorders do occur in children and adolescents.

Although you, as a parent, have probably known something was amiss with your teen that was more than just the normal storms of the teenage years, it has taken professionals many years of clinical review and scientific research to admit that teens, like adults, can be depressed. It was always much easier to say "it's just a passing phase" or "Don't worry—it will go away." But depression does not. Even when you can see teenagers bounce back, periods of depression do leave their marks.

Depression is painful. When a teen is suffering, they are no longer learning or growing. They can quickly fall behind their peers. They begin to act out their inner pain in various ways. Many people start labeling them as lazy, shy, or rebellious—names that stick and that soon become self-fulfilling prophesies. If depression is left unchecked, teenagers may be inappropriately placed in a classroom for learning disabled youth or, worse, in a juvenile detention center. At this point, their self-esteem has suffered irreparable damage because they see themselves as failures or stupid or they feel isolated and think that no one can possibly like them.

There is no denying that many adolescents go through times of despair, loneliness, or share their intense disappointment or rage. Teenagers react, and sometimes overreact, to perceived humiliation and setbacks. They also tend to be impulsive and rarely have the perspective that comes with age.

However, once in a depressive cycle, it is hard to get out. It can become like a bad habit—a continuous saga of negative self-statements, rotten feelings, and urges to die.

The book was not written to make you think that you must seek psychiatric treatment for all teenagers—most teenagers do get along, at least reasonably well, with parents, teachers, and peers. The purpose in writing this book was to make you aware of certain facts and to make you an educated consumer of mental health services.

You should not have to feel helpless and ineffective when trying to obtain assistance for your children and your family. Everyone needs help and support at one time or another, especially during that part of the family life cycle dealing with raising teenagers—truly the hardest time to be a parent!

By reading this book, you have probably discovered that there are many stories of teenagers who are suffering and their parents who are worrying. And that there are many people who can and want to help, both professionals and nonprofessionals. They can be accessed through your schools, churches, doctors, and hospitals. Look in the phone book, talk to your neighbors. In this age of computers, there are even electronic networks for parents to share their experiences of dealing with the special needs of their children.

Yes, this is a different age, but there has always been that time between childhood and adulthood that makes parents nervous. Socrates, around 400 B.C. described the youths of his time as "tyrants." Ancient carvings from 4,000 years ago have revealed civilization's problems with teenagers— "Civilization will be doomed if the actions of our younger generations are allowed to continue."

Although few would have envisioned the problems of present times, certainly teenagers have always been seen as being in the middle of conflict. You are not alone in your wonderment at their energy, creativity, and destructiveness. But maybe now you are closer to saying that you understand.

Organizations and Support Groups

American Association of Suicidology
2459 S. Ash Street
Denver, CO 80222
(303) 692-0985
Clearinghouse on topics related to suicide. Provides nationwide referrals to hotlines and support groups. Will mail free pamphlets.

Children with Attention Deficit Disorders
1859 N. Pine Island Rd., Suite 185
Plantation, FL 33322
(305) 587-3700
Provides listing of self-help support groups across US that meet on a monthly basis to offer information, experts, and support to parents of hyperactive children.

Depression and Related Affective Disorders Association, Inc.
c/o Johns Hopkins Hospital, Meyer 4-181
1601 N. Wolfe Street
Baltimore, MD 21205
Group of patients, families, and professionals concerned about clinical and manic depression; offers education, support, and treatment alternatives. Newsletter *Smooth Sailing* published quarterly.

National Alliance for the Mentally Ill
2101 Wilson Blvd., Suite 302
Arlington, VA 22201
(703) 524-7600
A self-help, advocacy organization for individuals with serious mental illness and for their families and friends. Provides mutual support groups, public advocacy, research, lobbying, and lists of local groups.

National Clearinghouse on Family Support and Children's Mental Health
c/o Portland State University
PO Box 751
Portland, OR 97207-0751
(800) 628-1696
Assists families of children with serious emotional disturbance and also aids mental health care professionals. Maintains state-by-state resource file.

National Committee on Youth Suicide Prevention
825 Washington Street
Norwood, MA 02062
(617) 769-5686
Volunteer network of parents and professionals who offer advice on preventing suicide among youth.

National Families in Action
2296 Henderson Mill Road, Suite 300
Atlanta, GA 30345
(404) 934-6364
Fax: (404) 934-7137
Group of volunteers who sponsor the National Drug Information Center. Helps interested parents organize local groups against drug usage. Provides drug-related materials for schools and libraries, and publishes abstracts of current articles from the medical journals.

National Foundation for Depressive Illness, Inc.
PO Box 2257
New York, NY 10116
(800) 248-4344
Provides recorded messages about depressive symptoms and manic-depression. Includes instructions on how to receive additional information related to mood disorders.

Parents Involved Network
311 S. Juniper Street, Room 902
Philadelphia, PA 19107
(215) 735-2465
Helps parents of children with severe emotional problems. Provides forums and suggestions for coping.

Society for Light Treatment and Biological Rhythms
PO Box 478
Wilsonville, OR 97070
(503) 694-2404
Fax: (503) 694-2404
An organization of scientists, clinicians, and patients who are developing, evaluating, and providing light treatment for those suffering from seasonal affective disorder.

Teen Suicide Prevention Taskforce
PO Box 76463
Washington, DC 20013
(213) 642-6000
Maintains list of speakers and relevant publications. Assists suicide prevention programs.

Youth Suicide National Center
204 E. 2nd Avenue, Suite 203
San Mateo, CA 94401
(415) 347-3961
Helps community and state educational institutions establish prevention programs. Provides catalog of publications.

Selected
Bibliography
and Resources

FOR PARENTS

Books

Caron, A.F. (1994). *Strong mothers, strong sons: Raising adolescent boys in the 90s*. New York: Henry Holt.

DePaulo, J.R., and Ablow, K.R. (1989). *How to cope with depression: A complete guide for you and your family*. New York: Fawcett Crest.

Eastman, M., and Rozen, S.C. (1994). *Taming the dragon in your child: Solutions for breaking the cycle of family anger*. New York: John Wiley & Sons.

Meeks, J.E. (1988). *High times/low times: The many faces of adolescent depression*. Washington, DC: The PIA Press.

Mooney, B.T. (1993). *Leave me alone! Helping your troubled teenager*. New York: McGraw-Hill.

Parrott, L. (1993). *Helping the struggling adolescent: A guide to thirty common problems for parents, counselors, and youth workers*. Grand Rapids, MI: Zondervan Publishing House.

Shimberg, E.F. (1991). *Depression: What families should know*. New York: Ballantine Books.

Pamphlets

About suicide among young people. (1986). Available from Channing L. Bete, South Deerfield, MA 01373.

Depressive disorders: Causes and treatment. (1981). Available from National Institute of Mental Health, 5600 Fishers Lane, Rockville, MD 20857.

Jones, J. A. (1987). *Teen suicide: A guide to understanding adolescents who take their own life.* Available from Minerva Press, 6653 Andersonville Road, Waterford, MI 48095.

Oster, G. D. (1989). *About teenage depression.* Available from Winters Communication, 14740 Lake Magdalene Circle, Tampa, FL 33613.

Oster, G. D. (1989). *Preventing teenage suicide.* Available from Winters Communication, 14740 Lake Magdalene Circle, Tampa, FL 33613.

Sargent, M. (1986). *Depressive disorders: Treatments bring new hope.* Available from National Institute of Mental Health, 5600 Fishers Lane, Rockville, MD 20857.

FOR COUNSELORS AND EDUCATORS

Berman, A.L. and Jobes, D.A. (1991). *Adolescent suicide: Assessment and intervention.* Washington, DC: American Psychological Association.

Haley, J. (1980). *Leaving home: The therapy of disturbed young people.* New York: McGraw-Hill.

Kirk, W.G. (1993). *Adolescent suicide: A school-based approach to assessment and intervention.* Champaign, IL: Research Press.

Klerman, G. (1986). *Suicide and depression among adolescents and young adults.* New York: American Psychiatric Press.

Mirkin, M.P., and Koman, S.L. (Eds.). (1985). *Handbook of adolescent and family therapy.* New York: Gardner.

Mishne, J.M. (1986). *Clinical work with adolescents.* New York: Free Press.

Oster, G.D., and Caro, J.E. (1990). *Understanding and treating depressed adolescents and their families.* New York: John Wiley & Sons.

Pfeffer, C. (1986). *The suicidal child.* New York: Guilford Press.

Richman, J. (1986). *Family therapy for suicidal people.* New York: Springer.

Seligman, M.E.P. (1990). *Learned optimism: How to change your mind and your life*. New York: Pocket Books.

Shafii, M., & Shafii, S.L. (1992). *Clinical guide to depression in children and adolescents*. Washington, DC: American Psychiatric Press.

Singer, M.I., Singer, L.T., and Anglin, T.M. (Eds.). (1993). *Handbook for screening adolescents at psychosocial risk*. New York: Lexington Books.

Weiner, I.B. (1992). *Psychological disturbance in adolescence* (2nd ed.). New York: John Wiley & Sons.

Index